Walk Madeira

with

Shirley & Mike Whitehead

DISCOVERY WALKING GUIDES LTD

Walk! Madeira
First Edition published July 2006
Second Edition published May 2009
Third edition published November 2010

Copyright © 2010

Published by
Discovery Walking Guides Ltd
10 Tennyson Close, Northampton NN5 7HJ,
England

Maps
Maps sections are taken from **Madeira Tour &
Trail Map** 6th edition ISBN 9781904946571
published by **Discovery Walking Guides Ltd**.

Photographs
The photographs in this book were taken by the
authors and co-walkers.

Front Cover Photographs

The rocky outcrop of Pináculo
(Walk 32)

Contouring around
Pedra Riga (Walk 18)

Sub-tropical *laurisilva*
(Walk 15)

A solitary chapel, Cabo
headland (Walk 37)

ISBN 9781904946694

Walk! Madeira
CONTENTS

THE WALKS

WALKS IN FUNCHAL & THE CENTRAL REGION

WALKS IN THE SOUTH-EAST & NORTH-EAST REGIONS

WALKS IN THE CENTRAL EAST REGION

WALKS IN THE CENTRAL WEST REGION

WALKS IN THE SOUTH-WEST & NORTH-WEST REGIONS

THE AUTHORS

Shirley and Mike Whitehead settled in Madeira in 2002 and live in Jardim do Mar on the south west coast. Both born in Lancashire, England, they lived for many years in West Yorkshire where they pursued their interest in walking and the environment.

In his younger days, Mike spent many years living in Africa and together they have travelled overland through Lapland, Tanzania, Zimbabwe and Zambia undertaking walking and camping safaris in the Zambezi Valley, the Udzungwa Mountains and Chitwan National Park, Nepal.

Along with their Border Collie Lucy, they now spend much of their time discovering Madeira's diverse landscape and its natural and cultural history, not only walking the *levadas*, forest trails, moorland and mountain tracks and the coastal routes, but also visiting almost every town, village and hamlet across the island.

In undertaking the walking research for this publication they have surveyed and mapped all the included routes using satellite navigation equipment combined with cartographic software.

Shirley is a regular contributor to The Brit newspaper writing articles on walking and heritage and her first book **Shirley Whitehead's Madeira Walks** (ISBN 9781904946311) was published by Discovery Walking Guides Ltd in 2006.

Acknowledgements

Our sincere thanks to our co-walker Alan Wood, for all his help, enthusiasm and support and for his unceasing energy when tackling a number of the high altitude routes.

Many thanks also to Bill Couper and David Warwick for their valuable contributions.

Our thanks also to the following personnel of the Secretaria Regional do Ambiente & Recursos Naturais, Madeira:- for the help, encouragement and information received.
-       Dr. Nelio Silva - Director of Forestry Services
-       Dr. José Nunes - Funchal Ecological Park, and
-       Tourist Officers in Funchal and Ribeira Brava.

As a walker's paradise, Madeira has it all - majestic mountains, rugged coastline, ancient forests, a unique *levada* network and verdant flora; easy to see why so many walkers return to this beautiful island year after year. Over the past decade, the island's infrastructure and facilities have undergone extensive development; not least has been the substantial investment to improve walking trails helping make Madeira one of Europe's top hiking destinations. Twenty three routes across the island plus two new routes to be added in late 2010, have been designated 'Recommended Trails for Hikers' by the Regional Government, all being upgraded, signed and made safer for the public. This programme of 'Access for All' continues to increase the scope and variety of walking routes throughout the island, with a number now created specifically for disabled people, using the unique 'Joelette' cycles. One route for blind people and three additional routes for cyclists have been created; see Appendix B for details.

Walk! Madeira, the first publication to recognize this development, has been completely rewritten to incorporate all the official trails opened prior ro 2010 as well as a variety of alternative walking routes, which together range from gentle strolls to Alpine-style mountain challenges - so whatever your level of walking fitness and ability, Madeira offers an exciting experience.

All routes included have been surveyed and mapped using GPS satellite navigation. The authors and their co-walkers have walked all the trails between 2008 and 2010, ensuring accuracy and up to date information. Clear descriptions guide the walker both to the starting point of the walks and throughout the routes, with gradings, distances, timings and altitudes all symbolized. Information on flora and fauna is also included while references to places of interest give readers a sense of the culture and history around these trails. Map sections were developed from the **Madeira Tour & Trail Map**, by far the most up to date and best-selling map on the island.

ADVERSE WEATHER CONDITIONS IN MADEIRA

You may be aware that in February 2010 the island suffered from severe flooding and landslides causing many *levadas* and other walking routes to be temporarily closed. Most of these have now been reopened and made safe. Later in the year the island also suffered from extensive fire damage, closing a number of high altitude routes and those in the Funchal Ecological Park. Such occurrences are rare - the last flooding on this scale was over 200 years ago - however, due to the island's isolation in the Atlantic and its natural mountainous terrain, isolated problems do occur from time to time, albeit on a much smaller scale. Landslips and *levada* maintenance occasionally have the effect of closing routes; nevertheless Madeira is still a beautiful and safe destination for walkers.

We suggest that if in doubt before setting out on any trail, visitors should check with their hotel reception or the Tourist offices, all of which receive regular bulletins from the authorities and can advise on the current status of most routes. Those with access to a computer can find this information on the official tourism website:-

www.madeiraislands.travel/Madeira

Madeira is a wonderful destination for walkers offering a diversity of landscape that is truly breathtaking; its lushly vegetated slopes, towering volcanic peaks, dramatic gorges and valleys and soaring cliffs, all take visitors by surprise. Add to this its comprehensive *levada* system, the primeval forests and the subtropical flora - little wonder then that the island is often referred to as "The floating garden of the Atlantic".

Forested slopes seen from Pico Ruivo (Walk 20)

GEOGRAPHY

The archipelago is situated in the eastern Atlantic, 950 kilometres south of mainland Portugal and 600 kilometres west of Morocco. It consists of the principle island of Madeira, **Porto Santo**, the **Desertas** and the **Salvagens**; the latter two being uninhabited nature reserves protected by the Parque Natural da Madeira. Together with the Azores, Canaries and the Cape Verde Islands, these archipelagos form a bio-geographic region referred to as Macaronesia.

Madeira extends to 57 kilometres east-west and 23 kilometres north-south, with an area of about 737 square kilometres. The neighbouring island of **Porto Santo** (42 km^2) is renowned for its magnificent sandy beach. The central massif of Madeira includes the great peaks of **Pico Ruivo** (1862m), **Pico Areeiro** (1818m). **Pico das Torres** (1852m) and **Pico do Gato** (1782m). The north coast boasts steep, tall sea cliffs; the most extreme however is **Cabo Girão** on the south coast, being the highest in Europe and second highest in the world.

CLIMATE

Madeira enjoys a temperate climate throughout the year with average daytime temperatures around the coast of 18°C - 24°C. However, in common with many mountainous islands, Madeira experiences numerous micro climates within its broadly subtropical climate. Generally speaking, the north of the island is wetter and cloudier than the south, while along the island's roughly west-east mountainous spine, the weather is subject to rapid change and can be windy, wet and cloudy - and occasionally, snowy. Clouds often gather and winds increase as the day progresses, so if planning long or high level routes, it's best to start early.

There's a useful website (**www.netmadeira.com**) giving hourly updates on weather conditions across the island, via web cam photographs, an invaluable resource for checking coastal and mountainous areas before you leave base.

THE LEVADAS

Although irrigation channels are not unique to Madeira, the island undoubtedly boasts some of the world's finest examples. There are over 200 *levadas*, covering 1500 kilometres, and new channels are still being constructed. As soon as the early settlers began clearing terraced pockets of land on which to raise crops, they needed to guide the rainwaters to these areas, and so *levadas* began. It's thought that the first attempts in the 15th century were made from lengths of wood, gradually replaced with more durable and watertight stone channels. Newer versions are made from reinforced concrete.

A tunnel on Walk 1

Most slope gently - almost imperceptibly in some cases - as they follow the natural contours of the terrain, providing ideal walking where accompanying paths allow. Where the shape of the land gets in the way, tunnels have been pushed through to take the channels. In the last decades of the 20th century hydroelectric power stations harnessing the power of new high altitude *levadas* were built, now providing some 30% of the island's power. From the walker's point of view, the *levadas* not only provide memorable and beautiful walking experiences, they open up otherwise impenetrable regions of the island.

The *levada* at Lamaceiros, Walk 39

Levadeiros (Levada Workers) are charged with keeping the channels and pathways in good condition and the levada keeper's cottages, usually surrounded by well planted gardens, can be found along many of the routes.

FLORA AND FAUNA

The Laurisilva

The island's name means 'wood', so named by early settlers who found it almost totally covered by great forests of mainly Lauraceae species, but over the centuries the trees were used for timber and the lower woodlands were burnt to release land for farming and pastures. Newer forests of pine, acacia (Mimosaceae), eucalyptus and oak now occupy much of the *laurisilva's* former territory. Nevertheless, the natural forest of Madeira is the largest area of *laurisilva* in the world. It covers 150 sq. km (58 square miles) representing just over 20% of the island's surface. Many of the plants evolved millions of years ago and the *laurisilva* survives now only in Central Macaronesia. These subtropical humid forests influenced by the mist grow in the cloud zone at 300m - 1300m in the north and 700m - 1200m in the south. Due to their importance they were classified a World Nature Heritage Site in 1999 by UNESCO.

Plants and Trees

Given its climate and fertility, Madeira is a botanical paradise, renowned for its luxurious vegetation. The first species you are likely to notice on arrival are tropical palms and cycads (from around the world) together with the Swan's Neck Agaves (Mexico), profuse

Sword Aloe (Aloe arborescens)

Jacarandas in springtime Funchal

around the airport, and the Red Sword Aloe (S.Africa) flanking roadsides in winter.

Many introduced ornamental plants and trees are cultivated in parks, gardens and along roadside verges. Prolific and widespread are Agapanthus, Hydrangea (S. Africa), Bird of Paradise (strelitzia), Flamingo Flowers (Anthurium), Hibiscus, Bougainvillea, and Protea to name a few.

Strelizia reginae

In spring **Funchal**'s streets are adorned with avenues of flowering trees including the distinctive blue jacarandas (Argentina), pink flowering Kapoc Trees (Brazil), red Tulip Trees (Africa), Flame Trees (Australia) and yellow Pride of Bolivia (S. America), in turn providing a blaze of colour and contrast throughout the year.

There are over 1300 species of indigenous and naturalized plants of which 150 are endemic; of these perhaps the two varieties of Pride of

Echium Candicans

Madeira Orchid
(Orchis maderensis)

Madeira (Echium candicans and Echium nervosum) are most frequently seen, yet wild geraniums, orchids, Sow Thistles and the rare Yellow Foxglove (Isoplexis sceptrum)are also a joy to discover. The magnificent Macaronesian endemic Dragon Tree (Dracaena draco) is now almost extinct on Madeira; the only two surviving naturally are in **Ribeira Brava** though they can be seen in parks and gardens; there's also an impressive display at Núcleo de Dragoeiros das Neves Nature Centre near **São Gonçalo**. (See Appendix A for details).

Vineyards and banana plantations dominate the lower coastal areas and along the agricultural terraces you will find exotic fruit trees of papaya, fig, mango, avocado, orange and lemon. The main vegetable crops include sweet potato, beans, tomatoes and various types of brassicas.

Yellow Foxglove (Isoplexis sceptrum)

Bananas

Birds

Madeira is a principal European bird-watching destination holding a rich diversity of birds, including endemic species and sub-species, as well as some of the most threatened seabirds in the world. About 250 bird species and subspecies have been recorded within the archipelago though only around 42 breed regularly.

The only true endemics are the long-toed pigeon (Columba trocaz), which inhabits the laurisilva, and the zino's petrel (Pterodroma Madeira), breeding on the cliff tops. There are however a number of endemic sub-species such as the firecrest, chaffinch, blackbird and wagtail, as well as Macaronesian endemics including the canary, Berthelot's Pipit, plain swifts and blackcaps.

SPEA-Madeira - The Portuguese Society for the Protection of Birds and a partner of Birdlife International, has produced two maps covering bird life in the laurisilva and **Ponta do Pargo** IBAs (Important Bird Areas defined by Birdlife International). A third map has also been published covering the **Funchal** Ecological Park. Details are given in Appendix C.

Animals

There are no mammals other than bats occurring naturally, however those introduced include rabbits and goats and a number of small rodents such as rats and mice, and of course, domestic animals, sheep and cattle. Grazing land being rather scarce on Madeira, you will often find cattle roaming on the roads and moorland on the southern slopes of **Paúl da Serra**.

Monarch butterly

There are a number of reptiles (although thankfully no snakes) with the only endemic species being the Madeiran Wall Lizard (Teira dugesii).Insects include grasshoppers, crickets and migratory locusts, plus many butterflies; the beautiful Monarch, the largest species on the island and Madeira Brimstone and Madeira Speckled Wood the only endemics.

Aquatic mammals include a number of species of whales and dolphins, which can sometimes be observed from the coastal areas. Also worth a special mention is the endangered Mediterranean Monk Seal, now thriving around the **Desertas** islands and occasionally seen off the coastline. Of the Aquatic Reptilia, turtles are a thriving species and are quite commonly seen in the coastal waters. A number of companies offer specialized sailing for whale & dolphin watching as well as trips to **Cabo Girão** and the **Desertas** islands. (For contact details see Appendix A - Other Things To Do).

BEFORE YOU SET OUT

When to Walk

Bearing in mind the island's climate, and that it is extremely lush and green, it follows that you can expect wet days on any visit. If you want to do high altitude routes, it's advisable to go when it is drier, from April to September. Some *levada* walks are popular even in the rain, and frequently offer shade during the hotter months.

Trails and Paths

Terrain on the routes varies widely. Some *levada* walks, although long, are on flat, easy paths with negligible ascents and descents; others require far more concentration on narrow paths, perhaps with sheer drops or on slippery, poor surfaces. Some routes, crossing mountain pastures such as Walks 5 & 6 in the Ecological Park and Walk 12 & 13 'Caniçal routes' in the east of the island, follow faint trails often obscured by vegetation.

The steep nature of the island means that many downhill routes (for example, Walks 4 'Ecological Park to Monte', Walks 19, 21 'Pico Ruivo to Encumeada and Ilha' and Walk 39 'Fonte do Bispo to Ribeira da Janela'), put a lot of strain on knees that are not used to it.

The official "Recommended Walking Trails".

During the past few years there has been a substantial investment in the upgrading of walking routes and in the provision of new trails across the island. The Autonomous Region of Madeira, with support from the EU, has funded the development under the 'Tourmac' programme, a project also covering walking routes in two other Macaronesian regions, the Azores and the Canaries. For further information visit **www.tourmac.info** or **www.madeiraislands.travel**

Twenty three routes across Madeira, plus three on Porto Santo have been designated 'Recommended Routes for Hikers' and two new routes will be added in late 2010. All are being upgraded, signed and made safer for the public. The twenty three routes on Madeira, opened prior to summer 2010 are referred to in the index and the walk descriptions and referenced with PR numbers, in Portuguese meaning 'pequeno rota' (small routes). These trails are the responsibility of the Regional Director of Forestry Service and along with the other routes included in this book, have been surveyed with GPS Satellite navigation and walked during 2008/2009/2010.

A PR Route Information Panel

Significant features of the PR development include: reinstated pathways, bridges and stairways on the trails, plus the erection of safety fencing where necessary. Signing includes the erection of Information Panels at start and finish points, plus fingerposts and field codes markings along the routes;

the panels provide details of terrain, altitude, expected weather conditions, walking times etc.

The Forestry service welcome comments from walkers on any problems encountered on any of the routes. Contact can be made through the Tourist Offices or by emailing the department at:

A fingerpost for the PR12

drf.sra@gov-madeira.pt

Preparation

Be prepared - read through the walk description before you set out, and take note of the information bar for each route. If you are new to walking on Madeira, start with a shorter, easier route.

Exertion ratings range from 1 (easy) to 5 (strenuous); these are inevitably subjective - our 'strenuous' might be 'average' for those fitter (or younger) than we are. The time taken for each route is our own recorded time and does not include stops for taking photos or refreshments. Timings and distances on linear routes refer as follows:

1. One way, where there are options for private or public transport at the end of the walk or,
2. Return times for those routes requiring retracing our steps back to the starting point.

It's advisable to try one of our shorter routes first in order to compare your pace with ours, then adjust the time you need to allow accordingly. Distance is shown in kilometres, and ascents and descents in metres. Vertigo risk ranges from 0 (no risk) to 3 (high vertigo risk). Note that the vertigo risk often applies to only a short section of the route, although if you're a sufferer, this could feel like the longest few metres you've ever walked. (See symbols ratings guide).

Safety

Do take safety seriously:-

- If you find a route made impassable by, for example, a landslide, then turn back. Attempting to find your own way through can be highly dangerous, especially on newly fallen slides. Look for the signs; if the landslip has been levelled or boarded by the *Levadeiros*, then it is usually safe to cross.
- Take note of local weather forecasts (remember that weather changes happen swiftly on mountainous islands, especially at altitude).
- Start out early and plan to finish well before dusk. Let someone know (at your hotel, for example) where you plan to walk, and if possible walk with a companion. Bear in mind that mobile phones may not always work in remote parts of the island.
- Go properly equipped with an up to date map and guide book; a GPS is desirable but not essential; a compass at least is recommended.
- Clothing, including footwear, must be up to the job.

- advice on these and on other essentials are listed in the 'Walking Equipment' section.

Please note that there is no organized mountain rescue service in Madeira; incidents are dealt with by a combination of Ambulance, Fire and Police services. Whilst trails are "recommended" by the Regional Government, the information boards on the PR routes clearly state that "no responsibility whatsoever is accepted for personal injury or loss or damage of property by those walking the routes". We are individually responsible for our own safety, so should take adequate precautions and follow a common sense code. We suggest the following checklist:-

- Keep to the routes given
- Always let someone know where you are heading and your expected time of return.
- Wear suitable footwear and clothing
- Turn back if bad weather sets in and on no account attempt to cross newly fallen landslips
- Don't take risks
- Take lots of water with you, and food on longer walks
- Always carry ans use sun cream
- If possible, take a mobile phone and emergency contact numbers

GETTING AROUND

Hire cars and taxis are the most convenient way of getting around and, since the completion of the Rápida (VR1) and the other major (VE) highways, accessibility to all areas of the island is relatively quick and easy via a network of tunnels and bridges.

Hire cars at competitive rates, are available at the airport and from hotels and agencies in **Funchal**, as well as from other towns around the island. Taxis are another option at reasonable cost. Drivers will take you to the start of each walk and, if required, will collect you at the end. Taxis can be hired for half or full days and drivers carry standard price lists for journeys outside **Funchal**. See Appendix A for taxi phone numbers.

We recommend you make use of the excellent bus services. Bus journeys are an adventure, when you'll admire not only the high-up views of the scenery, but also the aplomb of the bus drivers who hurl their vehicles around impossible bends hanging over dizzying drops. Many of the walks in this book can be accessed by bus (see each walk's introduction) and there are special tickets that make this good value. We recommend the latest edition of Madeira Bus & Touring Map (Published by Discovery Walking Guides), invaluable for bus users and car drivers alike. Timetables can be purchased from bus and newspaper kiosks in **Funchal**. (See also Appendix D for Bus Information, including website address for two of the main operators on the island)

THINGS TO DO (OTHER THAN WALKING)

Madeira is justifiably famous for its wines, even to the extent of being mentioned by William Shakespeare. There are organised visits to some of the most famous wine producers premises with the inevitable tastings and encouragements to buy. Details from Tourist Offices. Madeira's markets are worth a visit, especially the one in **Funchal**, which is a riot of flowers, fruits and vegetables, fish and handicrafts.

Take a cable car ride, (the *Teleférico*) - there are now six operating around the island serving the following areas: -

- **Funchal**, sea front to **Monte**
- **Babosas** to the **Botanical Gardens**
- **Garajau** to the beachside complex -(besides the impressive statue of Christ, a replica of the Rio statue)

- **Achada da Cruz** to the *fajás* and vineyards at beach level
- **Rancho, Câmara de Lobos**, to the agricultural areas at sea level
- **Rocha do Navio, Santana** to the vineyards and islets along the coast
- **Cabo Girão** to **Fája dos Padros** (A lift rather than cable car), but a wonderful location for sun, sea, food and wine)

Go adventuring on the excellent buses. As well as accessing many of our walking routes, they make great sightseeing days out - at pocket money prices. See 'Getting Around', above..

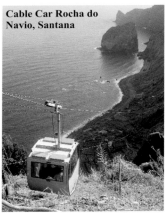

Cable Car Rocha do Navio, Santana

For other activities including, golf, horse riding, diving, sailing trips to the **Desertas** islands, whale & dolphin watching, fishing and bird watching (See Appendix A - Other things To Do).

Tourist Offices can provide details of the island's many museums. (The official Tourist Offices are shown at Appendix A).

SYMBOLS RATING GUIDE

our rating for effort/exertion:-
1 very easy **2** easy
3 average **4** energetic
5 strenuous

approximate **time** to complete a walk (compare your times against ours early in a walk) - does not include stopping time

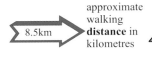

approximate walking **distance** in kilometres

250m
850m

approximate **ascents/descents** in metres (N=negligible)

circular route

linear route

figure of eight route

risk of **vertigo** - from 1-some risk to 3-high risk

refreshments (may be at start or end of a route only)

Walk descriptions include:
- timing in minutes, shown as (40M)
- compass directions, shown as (NW)
- heights in metres, shown as (1355m)
- GPS waypoints, shown as (Wp.3)

Notes on the text
Place names are shown in **bold text**, except where we refer to a written sign, when they are enclosed in single quotation marks. Local or unusual words are shown in *italics*, and are explained in the accompanying text.

MAP PROVENANCE

Simplified and adapted map data provided by Discovery Walking Guides Ltd. (copyright David Brawn) has been used to prepare this locator map.

The latest editions of Madeira Tour & Trail Map and Madeira Bus & Touring Map are available from:

www.walking.demon.co.uk
www.dwgwalking.co.uk

Digital mapping for a variety of destinations including Madeira is available from:

www.instant-books.org

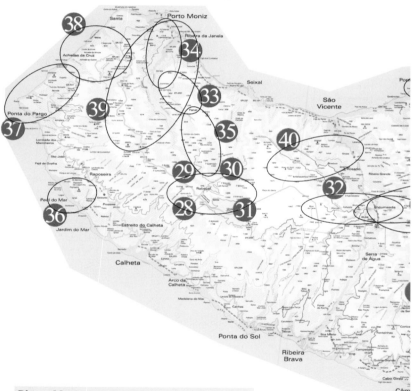

Please Note:

This locator map is intended to give a general indication of each walk area.

In order to avoid confusion, where two or more walks share a similar area, only one elipse common to that group has been drawn.

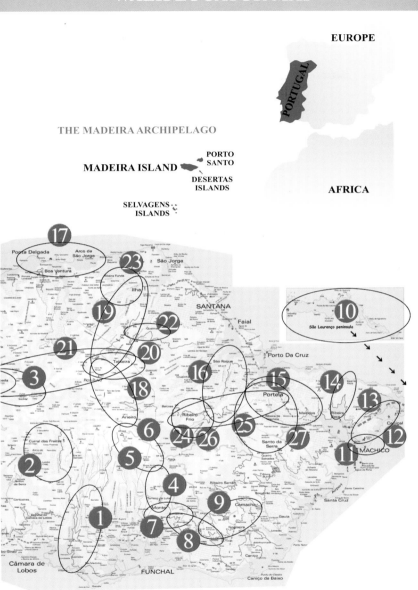

EUROPE

PORTUGAL

AFRICA

THE MADEIRA ARCHIPELAGO

MADEIRA ISLAND

PORTO SANTO

DESERTAS ISLANDS

SELVAGENS ISLANDS

The map sections in this book have been adapted from **Madeira Tour & Trail Map** published by **Discovery Walking Guides Ltd.**

Madeira Tour & Trail Map, and **Madeira Bus & Touring Map**, are available from:

Discovery Walking Guides Ltd.
21 Upper Priory Street
Northampton NN1 2PT

- or online at www.walking.demon.co.uk and www.dwgwalking.co.uk

Digital mapping for destinations including Madeira can be found at:
ww.instant-books.org

Madeira Tour & Trail Legend-Legende

ALTITUDE, HÖHE, ALTITUD, ALTITUDE

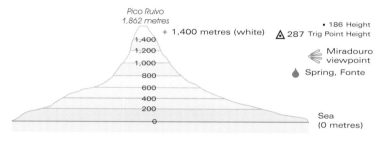

Pico Ruivo
1,862 metres

+ 1,400 metres (white)

1,400
1,200
1,000
800
600
400
200
0

• 186 Height
△ 287 Trig Point Height

Miradouro viewpoint

Spring, Fonte

Sea
(0 metres)

ROADS, STRAße, CARRETERA, ROUTE

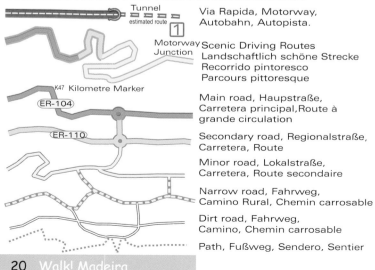

Tunnel

estimated route

Motorway Junction

K47 Kilometre Marker

ER-104

ER-110

Via Rapida, Motorway, Autobahn, Autopista.

Scenic Driving Routes
Landschaftlich schöne Strecke
Recorrido pintoresco
Parcours pittoresque

Main road, Haupstraße,
Carretera principal,Route à grande circulation

Secondary road, Regionalstraße,
Carretera, Route

Minor road, Lokalstraße,
Carretera, Route secondaire

Narrow road, Fahrweg,
Camino Rural, Chemin carrosable

Dirt road, Fahrweg,
Camino, Chemin carrosable

Path, Fußweg, Sendero, Sentier

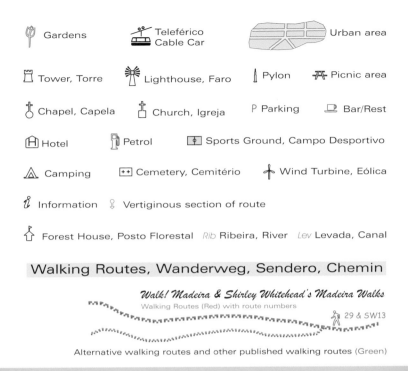

Gardens — Teleférico Cable Car — Urban area

Tower, Torre — Lighthouse, Faro — Pylon — Picnic area

Chapel, Capela — Church, Igreja — P Parking — Bar/Rest

Hotel — Petrol — Sports Ground, Campo Desportivo

Camping — Cemetery, Cemitério — Wind Turbine, Eólica

i Information — Vertiginous section of route

Forest House, Posto Florestal — *Rib* Ribeira, River — *Lev* Levada, Canal

Walking Routes, Wanderweg, Sendero, Chemin

Walk! Madeira & Shirley Whitehead's Madeira Walks

Walking Routes (Red) with route numbers

29 & SW13

Alternative walking routes and other published walking routes (Green)

USING GPS ON MADEIRA

GPS' 'pinpoint navigational accuracy' can be a great benefit for walkers, especially when tackling landscapes they have not seen before. The 5-metre accuracy achieved under good reception conditions can be a great confidence builder by knowing exactly where you are, especially useful for finding the start of walking routes after you have driven through Madeira's now extensive system of road tunnels and for knowing where you are on each walking route. Waypoints are included in the walking route descriptions as points where you either need to take a decision (e.g. path junctions) or for something you should see at that point in the walk. Its all too easy when walking to wonder if you have missed a junction, or are going the wrong way, but using a GPS along with our waypoints you will be reassured that you are both in the right place and going the right way - very reassuring for first time visitors (and regular visitors) to Madeira.

The GPS Waypoint Lists provided in this **Walk! Madeira** 3rd edition guide book by Shirley and Mike Whitehead, are as recorded during the research of the main walk descriptions contained in this book plus a number of detailed road surveys conducted to update our Tour & Trail Map of the island. Each waypoint symbol shown on the map for each walk is numbered so that it can be directly identified against the walk description and waypoint list.

All the GPS waypoints quoted in Walk! Madeira 3rd edition were recorded during Shirley and Mike's research of the walking routes, and are subject to the general considerations as to the accuracy of GPS units in the location concerned. Poor GPS reception will be encountered in the bottom of steep barrancos and ravines where your GPS can only see the satellites directly overhead, in dense woodland when the tree trunks and branches block the satellite signals, while vertical cliff faces (combined with Madeira's magnetic rock) and buildings can result in reflected signals giving confusing results for your GPS. Where we encounter poor reception then usually there is only one obvious walking route; such routes include:-

- **Walk 7** between the waterfall and **Romeiros** along (or in) the *levada* clinging to the cliff face.
- **Walk 15** in sections of the dense woodland.
- **Walk 25** along the **Levada do Furado**.
- **Walk 27** in the dense woodland alongside the *levada*.
- In the steep ravine at **Rabaçal** and at the source of the **Levada da Ribeira da Janela**.
- In any tunnels when you will get nil GPS reception.

It is virtually impossible to reproduce the exact GPS waypoint co-ordinates in practice when walking a route. While we quote GPS waypoints to 00.0001 minutes of arc, in practice you should expect 10 metres as an acceptable standard of accuracy when you have '3D navigation' (four or more satellites in view). The object of waypoints is to tell you when you need to take a decision (which trail to take) or for something you should see; used with the detailed walk description you'll find that GPS enhances your walking experience.

Signal Strength
Signal strength from sufficient satellites is crucial to obtaining an accurate location fix with your GPS unit. In open sky, ridge top, conditions you may have up to 11 satellites in view to give you a GPS location accuracy of 5 metres. Providing you have good batteries, and that you wait until your GPS has full 'satellite acquisition' before starting out, your GPS will perform well on Madeira for the majority of our walking routes.

To Input the Waypoints
GPS waypoint co-ordinates are quoted for the WGS84 datum, in degrees and minutes of Latitude and Longitude. To input the waypoints into your GPS we suggest that you:-

- switch on your GPS and select 'simulator' mode or 'operate with GPS off' depending upon which GPS model you are using.

- check that your GPS is set to the WGS84 datum (its default datum) and the 'location format' 'hddd°.mm.mmm'.

- input the GPS Waypoints into a 'Route' file (note this is the Route in your GPS, a collection of Waypoints, and should not be confused with a walking route description) with the same number as the walking route number; then when you call up the 'Route' on Madeira there will be no confusion as to which walking route it refers to.

- repeat the inputting of routes until you have covered all the routes you plan to walk, or until you have used up the memory capacity of your GPS; even the most basic of GPS units will store up to 20 GPS Routes of up to 50 waypoints for each GPS Route, and you can always re-programme your GPS while on Madeira.

- turn off your GPS.

When you turn the GPS back on it should return to its normal navigation mode.
Note that GPS waypoints complement the detailed walking route descriptions in Walk! Madeira and are not intended as an alternative to the detailed walking route description.

Personal Navigator Files (PNFs) CD
Edited versions of the original GPS research tracks and waypoints are available as downloadable files on our PNFs CD. In addition to Madeira the CD contains Tenerife, La Gomera, La Palma, Lanzarote, Mallorca, Menorca, Brittany, Calais and Boulogne, Andorra, Axarquia, Aracena and Alpujarras; plus GPS Utility Special Edition software and all of our Walk! UK series of guidebooks. See DWG websites for more information:

www.walking.demon.co.uk & www.dwgwalking.co.uk

Confused by GPS?
If you are confused by talk of GPS, but are interested in how this modern navigational aid could enhance your walking enjoyment, then simply seek out a copy of GPS The Easy Way, the UK's best selling GPS manual. Written in an easy to read and lively style and lavishly illustrated, GPS The Easy Way takes you through all aspects of GPS usage from absolute basics up to GPS Expert and debunking the myths about GPS along the way, an essential purchase for anyone thinking of buying a GPS.

"A compass points north"
but
"A GPS tells you where you are, where you have been, and can show you where you want to go."

"Ask not 'What is GPS?' - ask 'What can GPS do for me?' "

GPS The Easy Way (£4.99) ISBN 9781904946229 is available from bookshops, outdoor shops, over the internet, and post free from:

Discovery Walking Guides Ltd.
10 Tennyson Close
Northampton NN5 7HJ
www.walking.demon.co.uk & www.dwgwalking.co.uk

Many visitors using this book will be regular walkers with experience of different terrains and extremes in temperature. The following information is offered as a checklist to those walking on Madeira for the first time.

Backpack

The weather in Madeira can be extremely hot, particularly in summer, so avoid carrying unnecessary weight. A 25-30 litre day pack should easily cope with all the equipment you will need for a day's walking. A ventilated back panel and a stand-off frame is best for ventilation and will be much more comfortable on hot days and on tough routes

Footwear

Do not compromise on footwear. While there are many comfortable paths on the island, a lot of the walking is on hard rock, and often on uneven surfaces. Choose between boots, shoes or sandals (tough, rugged, walking sandals).

Sun Protection

Always carry a comfortable sun hat, also useful should it rain. Choose a design that gives you plenty of shade, is comfortable to wear, and stays on your head in windy conditions. UV rays are more intense at high altitude, so sunglasses and high-factor sun cream are highly recommended.

Water & Food

You'll need plenty of water; a couple of half litre bottles, is the minimum, and add another couple for more demanding routes. You should also pack sufficient food for the longer trails.

Medical Kit

A small first aid kit may prove useful; add lip salve, a life saver in hot dry conditions, and tweezers to deal with splinters or cactus spines.

Navigation

Many of the routes, particularly if following *levada* channels, prove no problem for navigation; if you don't leave the path, you can't possibly get lost. However, we advise that you always carry your guide book and a good map. A compass is also useful to orientate yourself at the start of a route and for general directions, while a GPS unit is especially valuable on 'off the beaten track' routes (see section on Using GPS on Madeira).

Clothing

Choose loose comfortable clothing and add a lightweight waterproof jacket to your back pack; Madeira is famous for both sunshine and copious rainfall. Pack extra layers, especially when walking at higher altitudes.

Other Equipment

You definitely need a torch for all routes with tunnels; also remember spare batteries. A mobile phone and emergency numbers are recommended, although there are areas where reception is poor or even nil. Walking poles are an advantage, particularly on routes with steep descents. A whistle will attract attention if you get into difficulties.

The winged bridge

The **Socorridos Valley** is our destination for this varied trail which is close to the city yet offers delightful *levadas*, unique rural areas, a spectacular gorge and exciting tunnels. Our trail follows the **Levada do Curral** to the abandoned hamlet of **Fajã** in the **Ribeira da Lapa** gorge, later descending through **Pinheiro das Voltas** to pick up **Levada dos Piornais** and ending close to the magnificent winged bridge on the **Via Rápida**. This 'must do' route provides a wonderful introduction to the delights of Madeira walking, although sure-footedness and a head for heights are essential.

Tackle it in either direction; for those based in **Funchal**, it can be extended by picking up **Levada dos Piornais** close to the **Barreiros Stadium** and following the channel through the agricultural zone running above the **Lido** area to reach **Quebradas**. Allow an additional 75 minutes walking time for this option.

N.B. A guide user reported at the start of October 2010 that this route was still undergoing repair following the landslides earlier in the year. He did not feel confident that the route was safe to walk yet. As we go to press, repair work is ongoing so the situation is improving daily; however we advise that you enquire at the tourist offices on arrival before attempting this route.

Access by hire car or taxi: Madeira Shopping car park entrance, beside the tower advertising 'Burger King'

Access by bus: town buses N°s 8, 16 & 50 to **Madeira Shopping**, return bus N°2 from **Quebradas/Santa Rita**.

Leaving the shopping centre car park (Wp.1 0M), we cross over the road and drop down to a roundabout (Wp.2 2M) where we turn right to pick up the **Levada do Curral**, running alongside the road. Two minutes later, our route meets a junction with a narrow path on the left, which descends between banana plantations and a house with an aviary (Wp.3 5M). This is our route for the second section of the trail, but for now we continue alongside the *levada* as it begins to swing right before crossing a narrow section of shoulder.

Gardens before Wp.4

Passing through banana plantations dotted with houses, the channel soon veers left crossing a small bridge and continues to meander through this rural area chequered with agricultural plots, cottages and pretty gardens, leading us around the shady head of **Ribeira do Arvoredo** (Wp.4 20M).

Eventually leaving the houses behind, we find ourselves on the edge of the **Socorridos** valley where a dramatic change in scenery unfolds

A few metres along, a red warning sign appears on our right (Wp.5 35M), but we can continue ahead with care and, after passing a very short precarious section with broken fencing, the channel then flows through denser vegetation following the contours of the valley.

The tunnel at Wp.7

Beyond this point, the longer precipitous sections have been protected with sturdy railings (Wp.6 40M), making progress much safer and as we progress along, passing through a rock cutting, we arrive at a short tunnel (Wp.7 45M), which we can either stoop through or skirt around.

Now the magnificent slopes of the **Ribeira dos Socorridos** valley encircle us and, with the **Ribeira da Lapa** and **Curral das Freiras** gorges straight ahead, we head up the valley towards the abandoned hamlet of **Fajã**. To our left, a huge waterfall plunges hundreds of feet down the cliffs. Although man made to feed the hydropower station in the valley bottom, it nevertheless makes an impressive sight.

.. quaint cottages ..

A short distance ahead, we find signs of cultivation as we pass two quaint cottages (Wp.8 55M), where the *levada* is framed with trellises and vines. The only sign of life (when we've done the route) is a barking dog and washing hung out to dry; quite fascinating in this wild and isolated location. Soon after we reach a gateway across the channel (Wp.9 60M) and, after passing through a longer rock cutting, we find ourselves at the **Ribeira da Lapa** gorge. Water drips from the rock face onto the *levada* and from this point we can see the escarpment ahead with the waterfall cascading over the basalt cliffs, forming rainbows in the mist (Wp.10 70M).

It's now time to turn around and retrace our steps as the route from here becomes extremely hazardous. Looking ahead, we see a short staircase rising up the side of the escarpment; this leads into a tunnel and exits on the opposite side of the gorge. From here the channel skirts the hamlet and continues on its increasingly dangerous course into the **Curral Valley.** At the time of our survey, a landslip was clearly visible on this path, so it is definitely not recommended to go beyond this point.

With different perspectives on our return route, we now make our way back towards **Madeira Shopping** to begin the second section of our trail, taking the narrow path of **Travessa do Pinheiro das Voltas** between the banana plantation and the house with the aviary (Wp.3 135M) which leads between the plantations before becoming a narrow tarred lane bordered by pretty houses. Soon arriving at a T-junction with the **Pinheiro das Voltas** road (Wp.11 140M), we turn right in front of a snack bar and head down the road for around 350 metres before picking up a concrete track leading off to the right (Wp.12 148M). We follow this to its end where we descend a series of stone steps leading off to the left (Wp.13 150M).

The steps descend 60 metres through more plantations and indigenous vegetation before passing an impressive rock face, to arrive on to the shoulder of **Levada dos Piornais** (Wp.14 162M). We are high above the industrial complex and noisy rock-crushing plant where we are treated to an impressive exhibition of water engineering with tunnel sections. The channel flows across an aqueduct but appears to be built on thin air, the short tunnels linked by seemingly impossible sections of *levada* (all railed).

Entering the tunnel section

To negotiate these we must crouch and crawl under the low arches; once through, the excitement and exhilaration will make you want to go back and do it all over again. If you doubt your ability to traverse the tunnels, then take the alternative concrete steps at either end of the tunnel section to descend to the valley floor and ascend at the opposite end (Wp.15 168M). Take your choice, but, if you have come this far and can do the tunnels, you won't forget the experience.

Following the channel, it is now less than one kilometre before we arrive at an information panel above the **Via Rápida**, just east of the winged bridge; a spectacular sight from this elevation (Wp.16 176M). The channel is adequately protected along this stretch except for a 50 metre section, so if in doubt, either walk inside the channel or with one foot on each side until the rails resume.

Alternative
Another option is to start the route at this information panel, following it in the opposite direction. Access to this point by car is through the village of **Lombada**, the road to which is signed 'Local Access' from a new roundabout located 4 kilometres from the **Lido** area along **Estrada da Monumental**, the regional road linking **Funchal** to **Câmara de Lobos**. From the information panel, our final stretch of the walk begins across the tarred **Lombada** lane.

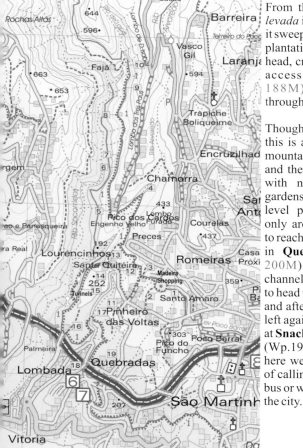

From this point on, the *levada* is covered over as it sweeps through banana plantations and at the head, crosses the valleys access road (Wp.17 188M) to continue through the plantations.

Though close to the city this is a pretty area; the mountains are in view and the *levada* is dotted with neat houses and gardens. On this good level path, it takes us only around 35 minutes to reach the regional road in **Quebradas** (Wp.18 200M). Leaving the channel here, we turn left to head up the main street and after 90 metres, turn left again to end the walk at **Snack Bar Santa Rita** (Wp.19 205M). From here we have the option of calling a taxi, taking a bus or walking down into the city.

2 EIRA DO SERRADO TO CURRAL DAS FREIRAS (NUN'S VALLEY)

Curral das Freiras is a traditional rural settlement, founded in the 16th Century by nuns of the Convent of Santo Clara who fled from **Funchal** following an attack by pirates in 1566 and sought permanent refuge there. The land was given over to the sisters who erected the first church in the area and created the agricultural environment, which still remains today.

The village's thriving centre relies mainly on tourism: each November it hosts a Chestnut Festival which draws in tourists and local people from across the island; displays in the cultural and traditional customs of the village are staged, while throughout the festival and during the whole year you'll find chestnut soup, chestnut bread and cakes and chestnut liquor on the menus.

Southern view from Eira do Serrado

This short trail begins at **Eira do Serrado** which sits on an impressive ridge high above the valley of **Curral** offering stunning views in all directions. The **Estalagem** offers accommodation, a restaurant and bar and a large, well-stocked souvenir shop; there's also an amazing *miradouro* only five minutes walk away.

Looking down to Curral das Freiras

The walk follows an ancient cobbled trail which originally connected **Nun's Valley** to **Funchal** and the south, before the creation of roads in the late 1950s. The path descends 400 metres making easy bends down the mountainside, providing a most spectacular approach into the valley below.

Before embarking on the walk it's well worth spending a little time at this stunning location and in particular visiting the *miradouro* which is reached along a well-manicured path leading from the hotel; the views of the central mountain range are amazing, with the majestic mountains encircling the little village of **Curral** far below.

2   1¼ H   2.5 km   nil / 405m   2

Access by hire car or taxi: leave **Funchal** via **São Martinho** heading for **Pico dos Barcelos**. Continue on the ER107 for around 10 kilometres, eventually meeting the new road and tunnel which descends into the **Curral** valley. For the start of the walk, turn left before the tunnel entrance, signed 'Eira do Serrado', parking at the **Estalagem** car park.

Access by bus:
Horário bus N°81 operates between **Funchal** and **Lombo Chão** in the **Curral** valley, also serving **Eira do Serrado**.

Heading for the point where the road enters the hotel car park, we descend a flight of steps leading down behind the building (Wp.1 0M) first passing through an area of chestnut woodland, characteristic of this location.

Sweet Chestnut (Castanea sativa)

The Sweet Chestnut (Castanea sativa), a genus of Fagaceae, the Beech Family, is cultivated both for its appearance and for the economic value of the fruit and timber. Originating from Europe and West Asia, it has naturalized across the island and is particularly prevalent in the **Curral** valley.

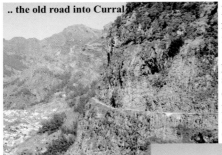
.. the old road into Curral

Descending the path, the old road into **Curral** soon comes into view on the right (Wp.2 8M), where it is carved on a precarious ledge against the steep rock face and snakes down the mountainside passing through tunnels along its descent. Continuing down the pathway, we take

Pico Grande

in wonderful views of **Pico Grande** (Wp.3 20M) with its unmistakable rocky stack at the summit before eventually reaching an exposed rock projection (Wp.4 35M), which offers good views down the valley and is a lovely place to stop for a rest.

The natural flora along this route includes Carline Thistles, Madeira Mountain Stock, marigolds, geraniums and one or two rare orchids, as well as the huge Black Parsley and Sow Thistles, all of course depending on the time of year visited.

The final stretch of the walk runs alongside the cultivated terraces before beginning a short ascent through the woodland, which in early spring, is carpeted with lovely yellow Celandines. After a total walking time of 1 hr 15 min, we reach the end of the trail as we arrive at a picnic table just above the ER107 road (Wp.5 75M). Turning right here, it is approximately 1 kilometre into the village centre where we can enjoy a drink or refreshments in one of the many cafes and bars and from where buses or taxis are available to take us back to **Eira do Serrado** or **Funchal**.

This beautiful mountain walks crosses part of the Central Mountain Massif running along the foot of the highest peaks. The pathway, known as the old Royal Path, once served as a main route for the island's inhabitants who moved on horseback between north and south. The trail has an initial ascent of 80 metres, the remainder undulating between elevations of 1340 and to 940 metres. The landscape is characterized by wild mountainous terrain, later entering into dense vegetation iincludeing many laurisilva species and, due to the stark variation in vegetation and terrain, many island bird species including buzzards, kestrels and the Madeira long-toed pigeon as well as firecrests, finches and wagtails.

Access by car or taxi: follow the ER229 via **Estreito de Câmara de Lobos** to **Jardim da Serra**. The road continues to climb, eventually reaching **Boca da Corrida** forestry post, a total of 10.2 km from the VR1.

Access by bus: Nº 96 serves **Corticeiras** and **Jardim da Serra**. It is then around 4 kilometres with a 350 metres ascent to **Corrida**; taxis are obviously the best option. There's a limited service via **Encumeada** on bus Nºs 6 & 139, serving **Serra da Água** and **Santa**, **Porto Moniz**. However, more frequently, these services travel from **Ribeira Brava** to **São Vicente** along the VE4 via the **Encumeada** tunnel.

The walk starts from the car park at **Boca da Corrida** Forestry Post, lying on a mountain ridge above **Estreito da Câmara** de **Lobos**. The house (at 1235 metres above sea level) is surrounded by sweet chestnut and conifer woodland. Within its confines is a lovely shrine dedicated to **São Cristovão**. Close to the car park we make a short detour to one of the most spectacular *miradouros* on the island before setting off on our trail.

Following the broad track beside the shrine, the walk officially begins at the information panel (Wp.1 0M). But first of all, don't miss out on the *miradouro*, which goes off right from the car park, following a narrow path leading to a grassy outcrop (Wp.2 3M). The views are magnificent and set the scene for what we are about to encounter along this trail. The north eastern vistas take in all the highest peaks as well as the great depression of **Curral das Freiras** (Nun's Valley), where the parish can be seen scattered along the valley floor. To the south lies **São Martinho** and the coast of **Funchal** whilst looking north-west, **Pico Grande** dominates the skyline.

Back at the information board, we climb a series of steps leading off the track to arrive at a fingerpost signed 'Encumeada 12.6 km' to start our initial ascent. After ten minutes we reach a ridge where the path levels out giving us a superb view of **Pico Grande**. Standing at 1657 metres, it towers ahead of us, its rocky castle-like formation unmistakable on the summit.

The trail follows the wide ridge, crossing a number of times from east to west and providing more wonderful views down the **Curral Valley** and across to the **Encumeada Pass,** where on clear das, the wind turbines on the **Paúl da Serra** plateau can be seen. The track passes a number of steep ravines,

The newly-laid steps at the start

... we start our initial ascent ...

many bearing a small copse of sweet chestnut trees bringing sharp relief to this barren mountainous landscape. Around 35 minutes later we pass a high rock wall on our left, where tree heaths and Echium candicans cling to the sloping hillside.

Now our trail begins its undulating route, passing another interesting rock face (Wp.3 40M) followed by a number of short descents and ascents which lead us to a ridge on the next hillside (Wp.4 45M) and from where we can see the stony descent of the track and the point where it crosses a natural land bridge at **Passo de Ares** (Wp.5 55M) the narrow strip dividing the **Brava** and **Socorridos** river valleys. The views to the east and west are wonderful.

The Nun's Valley

Moving on, we traverse round a wide arc at the foot of **Pico do Serradinho**, the highest point on the route at 1340 metres, which overlooks **Nun's Valley**, before passing a number of rocky outcrops and then circling back westwards, where **Serra de Água** and **Vinháticos** come into view.

Long sections of gorse, broom and bracken follow, so dense that at times we appear to be passing through tunnels of vegetation; long trousers are definitely recommended for this walk. With further ups and downs and contouring around more valleys, we eventually find ourselves at **Boca do Cerro** below the impressive **Pico Grande**, where the trail ahead can be seen heading west and cutting through the dense vegetation at the base of the mountain (Wp.6 90M). At this point a path leads off sharp right; the original fingerpost appears to have disappeared, but a large arrow scratched on a rock indicates the direction. This leads to **Chão de Relva**, a small grassy plateau with a clump of sweet chestnut trees from where one pathway leads to the summit of **Pico Grande** (add 1.5 hours return) with another heading down into the **Curral Valley** (3 hours).

However we ignore this to continue on, skirting the awesome rock face as we head off in a westerly direction. The path along this section is narrow, rocky and wet and also subject to rock falls, so caution is needed. Nevertheless it is quite good underfoot and dense vegetation provides us with lots of protection. Negotiating this escarpment takes around thirty minutes after which the trail begins its long descent to **Encumeada**, passing though forested areas before emerging again onto the mountain slopes. Twenty minutes later we arrive at **Fenda do Ferreiro**, a rocky outcrop with fine views across to **Paúl da Serra** (Wp.7 150M), a lovely place for a picnic.

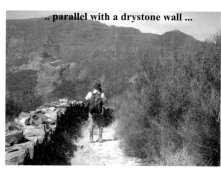
.. parallel with a drystone wall ...

Now beginning the steepest part of the descent, we soon pass under an unusual burnt tree (Wp.8 160M) after which the trail starts to zigzag and becomes very overgrown. Passing another spectacular viewpoint (Wp.9 180M), the paved path continues descending steeply before running parallel with a drystone wall.

Thirty five minutes later, a path leads off to the right, again more wonderful views (Wp.10 220M), but our route continues ahead leading us

down through a wooded area (Wp.11 235M) and crossing a number of river beds before arriving at a derelict building and a concrete bridge over a stream. A further eight minutes along we arrive at the **Grass Bridge** valley head in **Curral Jangão** (Wp.12 250M).

Now our trail climbs slightly under a canopy of trees, passing a derelict stone farm building on the left and old terraces to the right, before entering ancient woodland and crossing more rocky stream beds. Nearing the end of the walk we cross over the final riverbed with a waterfall to our right (Wp.13 295M) and contouring through eucalyptus woods, pass under a pipe (Wp.14 310M) carrying water from **Levada do Norte** down to the power station at **Serra da Água**. From here the path widens into a track where the **Residential Encumeada Hotel** comes into view on our left with the trail ending where it meets the ER228 (Wp.15 330M).

At the junction with the regional road we have the option of going right, to climb up to **Snack Bar Encumeada**, a distance of 500 metres, or going left for 1 kilometre, down to the **Residential Encumeada Hotel**.

The descent to Encumeada

The **Ecological Park** occupies an area of around 1000 hectares and is situated in the mountainous area above **Funchal**, extending at its most northerly point to **Pico Areeiro**. Created in 1994 with nature conservation as its prime objective, it offers environmental education and recreational facilities for residents and visitors.

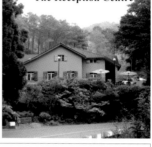
The Reception Centre

The Reception Centre at **Ribeira das Cales** houses a café and information centre and within the confines of the park, picnic and barbeque facilities can be found in picturesque settings. In addition there is a nursery for the production of indigenous plants; it's also the starting point for a number of adventurous outdoor pursuits such as mule trekking and canyoning.

Addendum October 2010

In August 2010 a series of fires raged over the central area of the island, badly affecting the forests and mountains; the Ecological Park was one of the worst hit areas, with around 95% of its vegetation damaged. Nevertheless, nature heals quickly and the undergrowth and low vegetation will recover well over the coming winter months, but unfortunately the forest trees may take many years. Immediate efforts are being made by the Government to redress the problems, particularly the habitats of rare and endangered species and also through a substantial increase in the production of nursery plants. As a result our descriptions for Walks 4, 5 & 6 will, in the short to medium term, differ from the actual condition of the park, but we believe that the routes, once reopened, will still provide stimulating walking opportunities.

This wonderful walk, starting from the Reception Centre descends two kilometers through the park before continuing on an ancient trail, an original footpath linking the north coast villages with **Funchal**. At around the halfway point the path emerges onto the regional road at **Terreiro da Luta** providing an opportunity to visit the statue of Our Lady of Peace, an historic monument erected in a superb elevated setting, giving fine views over **Funchal**. Our final section descends the famous **Calvario** route, passing a number of the stations of the cross before arriving in **Largo do Fonte** from where it skirts around the historic centre passing tropical gardens, palaces, the Church of **Nossa Senhora do Monte**, the toboggans and the cable car, before finally ending in the lovely **Babosas** square.

Very few walks on the island can boast such a wealth of interest in both the natural and built environment, thus providing something for every member of the family. This is one of the three recognized walking routes from the ecological park and has been newly reinstated to a high standard with yellow and red flash way markings clearly defined throughout.

Access by hire car or taxi: take the ER103 from **Funchal** passing through the centre of **Monte** parish and continuing in the direction of **Poiso**. The Reception Centre and car park at **Ribeira das Cales** are located approximately 5 kilometre north of **Monte** on the left of the road.

Access by bus: Funchal buses Nºs 21, 22 or 48 service **Monte**. Nºs 56, 103 or 138 serve the **Ecological Park**.

.. our walk begins ..

Our walk begins at a signpost at the rear of the reception centre (Wp.1 0M), which directs us down a flight of steps into the well planted gardens and leads us over a bridge to meet a junction where we continue ahead. Soon crossing a tarred forest road we pick up

the path on the opposite side and after one minute take a left turn at a T-junction. At the next junction we fork right to meet a cobbled road where we turn right before picking up the path again on the left a few metres along (Wp.2 7M).

The trail descends towards a fenced off pond supplying water for the park nursery, clearly visible from the cobbled path. Turning right immediately we reach the pond, we follow the path past the rear of the nursery where it becomes a little rocky underfoot before we climb a short flight of steps and pass through

On the woodland path

an area of large coniferous trees. Going right at the next junction (Wp.3 18M) and ascending for another few metres, brings us back to the cobbled road at a large picnic and barbecue site. Following left, we continue on a flight of paved steps and path ascending to a *miradouro* at **Pico Alto** (1129 metres Wp.4 27M). We can pause here to admire the fantastic view of **Funchal** as well as the surrounding mountain slopes, before leaving on the opposite side of the platform to take a narrow path left between a group of rock boulders.

Flanked by hydrangeas, this path leads us into the woodland following a gradual zigzag descent before straightening and levelling out, where we again glimpse the picnic sight, now at a higher level than us. Here we keep an eye out for a flight of steps to our right (Wp.5 34M) turning right again at the bottom. The path is rocky but level as it passes through the forest. Soon after it is joined by a gully (Wp.6 43M), from where it begins to descend. After skirting round two large boulders (Wp.7 47M), the descent steepens with more frequent flights of steps, before reaching the ER103 regional road (Wp.8 54M).

Leaving the forest, we continue on the opposite side of the road where we pick up the ancient cobbled pathway, alongside which runs **Levada das Cales**. Descending quite steeply, we soon arrive at a junction with the ER103 and ER201 regional roads at **Terriero da Luta**.

Our Lady of Peace

The path continues on the opposite side of the road, but we have an option here to leave our trail to visit the impressive monument of Our Lady of Peace; inaugurated in 1927, this five and half metre statue stands on columns looking south to the coast. It's reputed that the rosary at the base of the statue was formed from fragments of chain from ships sunk in **Funchal** harbour during the First World War which were transported manually during a pilgrimage to **Terreiro da Luta**. This landmark can be found 200 metres along the ER201.

Also of interest is the lovely **Quinta do Terreiro da Luta Restaurant**. Originally built as a rail station, it was the highest point of the **Monte** railway which closed in 1914. The station building has been restored and now houses a gourmet restaurant and the **Station Bar**. From the enchanting garden at the rear of the building there is a fantastic view of **Funchal** bay as well as an impressive bronze statue of João Gonçalves Zarco, Madeira's most important historical figure and founder of the island, which provides a wonderful centerpiece to this formal garden.

Optional detours aside and back on our trail, we continue on the ancient path going left beside the **Quinta** on **Caminho do Monte** (Wp.9 64M), descending a leafy lane to pass the 14th to the 6th stations of the cross which appear at intervals along the descent. After a few minutes we pass the Spring of the Shepherdess (Wp.10 70M), where in 1495 the Lady of Monte is said to have appeared.

A little further, we reach the first houses above **Monte** to pick up a tarred road for a few metres before rejoining the cobbled track again, signed 'Caminho das Lajinhas' (Wp.11 75M). From this point we leave the pilgrimage route as our path descends through an old area of **Monte**, passing between quaint rural houses and gardens as it twists and turns quite steeply before ending at a junction where two tarred roads meet. Crossing over, we pick up the trail again (Wp.12 85M) as we enter **Monte** gardens to arrive at the 1st station of the cross on the path above the village square.

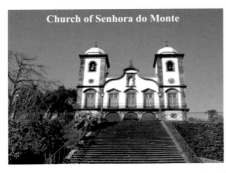
Church of Senhora do Monte

The route leads us around the Church of **Senhora do Monte** and as we approach the front we turn right behind a row of church cottages leading us gently down into **Largo do Fonte**. The bustling square exudes the charm of bygone days, with the bandstand, cafes, monuments, shrines and souvenir stalls to interest and amuse. Our final section takes us from the square along **Caminho das Babosas** (Wp.13 90M) passing **Monte Palace** Tropical Gardens on our right and soon arriving at the start of the toboggan run where white clad *carreiros* with their wickerwork sledges, make a splendid spectacle (Wp.14 95M).

Carreiros and toboggans

Following along the cobbled road, we pass the cable car station on our right (Wp.15) to end our walk in **Babosas** square (Wp.16 100M), dominated by huge plane trees and where we find the lovely chapel of **Nossa Senhora da Conceição**.

5 ECOLOGICAL PARK:

POÇO DA NEVE - CHÃO DA LOGOA - RIBEIRA DAS CALES
(PR 3 VEREDA DO BURRO)

This is the second of three official walking routes in the Ecological Park, both this and Walk 6 beginning at **Poço da Neve** on the northern boundary and descend almost its entire length. Of particular interest to bird watchers, both trails intersect with five ornithological routes which were signed and publicised in 2008. We recommend the map, 'Discover the Birds of the Funchal Ecological Park', available from the Reception Centre and bookshops. It is also an extremely good map for navigating the walking trails. See footnote for details.

Covering an area of 10 square kilometres, the park lies on the southern slopes of the eastern mountain range between 1818 and 500 metres altitude, providing diverse habitats and scenery. Walks 5 and 6 start in the high scrublands taking in pine, Eucalyptus and sections of indigenous forest on route, as well as water courses including streams and ancient *levadas* which pass through the park.

N.B. See Addendum 2010 - Walk 4 page 36.

Poço da Neve

Poço da Neve (the Ice House), was constructed from basalt chips in the shape of an igloo by Madeiran stonemasons. Financed by an Italian ice-cream maker, it was used from 1813 until the end of nineteenth century, to provide ice for the hospitals and for **Reid's Hotel**.

Access to this amazing and newly restored monument is by a narrow paved path leading from the road at the northern boundary of the park, from where there are uninterrupted views down the southern slopes to **Funchal** harbour.

Both trails are well signed throughout with red and yellow flashes and can be undertaken any time of year, but choose a clear day to take full advantage of the views. Note that these high altitude walks can be extremely cold and wet in winter; appropriate clothing and footwear are necessary. Walking poles are also an advantage on the steep descents.

Access: by hire car or taxi: the park is situated 5 kilometres north of **Monte**. For directions to the Reception Centre at **Ribeira das Cales**

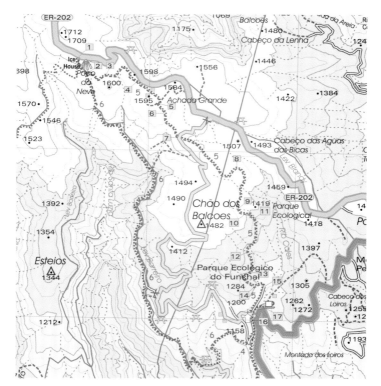

follow Walk 4. Walks 5 and 6 begin at the viewing area of **Poço da Neve** situated around 5 kilometres along the ER202 regional road between **Poiso** and **Pico Areeiro**.

Leaving the road (Wp.1 0M) we start at a junction just below the Ice House where a fingerpost signed 'Ribeira das Cales' directs us left over scrubland, followed soon by a second sign (Wp.2 13M) directing us left again to pass below **Pico dos Melros**. We now follow a wide track before our route turns right over a narrow grassy path heading towards two masts on the adjacent hillside (Wp.3 19M).

For about an hour our trail roughly follows the contours of the ER202. Look out for examples of a number of unique species of flora; Madeiran Mountain Ash (Sorbus maderensis), rare and closely protected, is found around **Pico dos Melros** and also alongside the regional road; a small perennial tree producing white flowers in summer and red berries in winter. Other species include Madeiran Holly (Ilex perado), ancient heaths, Giant Bilberry and Madeiran Grey Heather (Erica maderensis).

Following a short ascent we arrive at the old Metrological Station at **Casa do Areeiro** from where **Faial** and **Eagle Rock** are visible on the north coast (Wp.4 34M). In a few more metres we meet a vehicle track running in front of a utility tower where we turn right for a few metres before again taking a narrow grassy path on the left (Wp.5 43M). Crossing a grassy vehicle track (Wp.6 45M), our route now veers right on a path bordered by stones, from where **Funchal** can be seen in the distance.

A short descent follows, leading us to a water tank beside the municipal park road, where a large picnic and barbeque area sits on our right (Wp.7 56M). Crossing over and picking up our path again, we continue over a moorland area planted with small pines, two minutes later ignoring a turn-off left between bushes which heads towards a small valley and stream bed.

On reaching an open area we head left towards our next waypost (Wp.8 78M), which directs us down into the forest. Our route is now circling the recreational area of **Chão da Lagoa** and at this point we take a short detour to the right to take in a view of **Casa do Burro** before returning to the way post and following the path. Crossing two streams, the second over a flat wooden bridge (Wp.9 95M), we meet a junction in the path where our route goes left, the Ornithological Route 3 veering off right to end on the municipal road.

Beard moss (Usnea arida)

We find ourselves in coniferous forest mostly comprising pines completely covered in beard moss (Usnea arida), common in Madeira, where it thrives in humid and unpolluted areas. Underfoot, patches of Amanita muscaria, a large red and white toadstool, litter the woodland floor. This is said to be a poisonous plant, although psychoactive and used as an intoxicant in other cultures.

Amanita muscaria

We now descend a craggy path crossing over a narrow *levada* (Wp.10 102M), before stopping at a viewpoint looking across the forest and towards the coast and **Funchal**. Now the main descent begins on a steep and uneven stairway making progress quite slow, but it is not dangerous and galvanized rails and straining wires have been provided for support.

Towards the bottom the trail re-meets with the *levada* (Wp.11 119M), which we now follow almost to the end of our route. Scrambling over a large boulder, we arrive in an area of bramble, bracken and willows where the water channel suddenly widens into a small stream and a pretty waterfall appears on our right.

The trail continues from here alongside a ridge with a deep-forested area below us (Wp.12 130M). During the first two centuries of occupation the natural forest on the southern slopes of the island was devastated by fire and de-forestation, native trees being replanted with conifers, Eucalyptus, Acacias and Sweet Chestnuts, all of which are fast growing but not as effective in stopping erosion as are the native species. Consequently since the creation of the park in 1994, a programme of replanting native trees has been in place. Now entering an area of thriving young beech trees, (Wp.13 136M) we soon reach a junction from where the Reception Centre at **Ribeira das Cales** is visible below us (Wp.14 144M). Crossing over and descending more log steps and scrambling under a huge fallen pine, we then arrive at a wide forest track with a rustic gate and fencing to our left (Wp.15 152M)

Turning right here, the track soon becomes cobbled, and to our left the donkey stables come into view (guided rides cost from €5 to €25 to observe birds and flora). A few minutes along, the trail joins with the tarred municipal road which we descend and, just prior to reaching the southern gate at the regional road (Wp.16 159M), we turn left to head through the gardens along a paved path, crossing a bridge over **Ribeira das Cales** and climbing steps up to the Reception Centre, where we end the walk (Wp.17 165M).

The donkey stables

Bird Watching
The map of the Ornithological Routes was produced by Funchal City Council and sponsored by the Parque Ecological do Funchal, SPEA and BirdLife International. The publication identifies five bird watching routes at varying altitudes, and describes the four major habitats of exotic forest, streams, indigenous forest and high level vegetation and the species that can be spotted in each.

This walk, also starting at **Poço da Neve**, follows **Levada do Barreiro** on its descent to **Casa do Barreiro** in the south of the park. The *levada* runs along the eastern ridge of the **Ribeira de Santa Luzia** valley providing spectacular views along the way and finishing at **Ribeira das Cales**. This is another trail of particular interest to bird watchers as it too intersects with four of the ornithological routes.

Levada do Barreiro

The route, well way marked throughout, has a number of precipitous sections along **Levada do Barreiro**. While these are protected with galvanized rails and straining wire, they may cause vertigo for some people.

For information on the characteristics of the park, in particular the bird life and flora, refer to the details given in Walk 4 and 5.

N.B. See Addendum 2010 - Walk 4 page 36.

Access by Hire Car or Taxi; follow directions for Walk 5.

Leaving the **Poço da Neve** viewing platform (Wp.1 0M), we pick up the trail a few metres beyond at the first fingerpost directing us straight ahead and signed 'Levada do Barreiro' and 'Casa do Barreiro'. At the second signpost the paths fork (Wp.2 5M); from here our route heads off right through the heaths below **Pico dos Melros**, soon crossing a vehicle track before reaching the narrow water channel of **Levada do Barreiro** (Wp.3 13M). Our route is now running parallel to the *levada* until we reach **Casa do Barreiro**.

Passing a pine grove a little further along, the channel soon begins to fall and we follow its descent on a log stairway where care is needed, as the steps are very steep and slippery. On reaching the bottom (Wp.4 21M) we cross a rickety bridge over a stream bed, and veering off right, make another short descent, at the bottom of which is another rickety bridge (Wp.5 34M). A finger post appears here on our left (Wp.6 45M) for a path leading off to **Chão da Lagoa**, but we ignore this and continue, soon crossing a stream bed, a tributary of the **Santa Luzia** river, where we have our first views across the valley (Wp.7 52M).

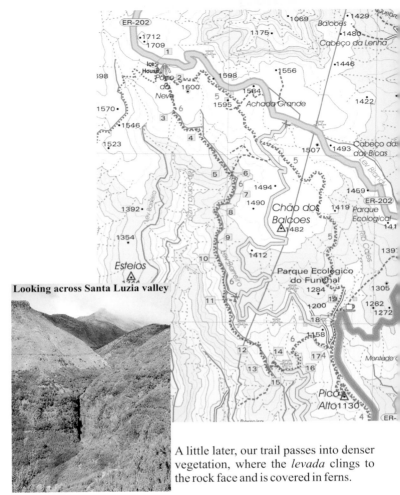

Looking across Santa Luzia valley

A little later, our trail passes into denser vegetation, where the *levada* clings to the rock face and is covered in ferns.

From hereon the channel shoulder becomes exposed in a number of places (Wp.8 59M); although handrails provide some protection, great care is needed at these points. Nevertheless, the mountain views across the valley are quite spectacular with the heather covered slopes broken by a number of fissures where beautiful waterfalls plunge into the valley below.

Another track now leads off left for a short detour; red arrows painted on a rock direct the way (wp.9 72M). This leads to a wonderful viewpoint and is a lovely place for a rest and lunch. Back on the main track, two impressive tree roots block the path (Wp.10 82M) followed by a third path leading off left (Wp.11 92M); this being a short cut back to the **Reception Centre**. Again we ignore this and continue to stay with the *levada*.

Another short, steep descent follows. At the bottom (Wp.12 108M) we cross to the left of the channel, two minutes later crossing back to the right and following a final descent on log steps, again steep, we drop onto a cobbled road (Wp.13 115M). Crossing over and continuing to follow the *levada* through an area of acacias with the occasional oak, the path swings left crossing over two small wooden bridges (Wp.14 124M) to arrive at a covered barbeque and picnic area at **Casa do Barreiro** (Wp.15 128M), the most southern of the park houses.

The final section of the trail leads us north to **Ribeira das Cales** and from the end of the forest house driveway, we lead off left in the direction of **Pico Alto** (Wp.16 133M). After crossing over a precarious bridge we negotiate a steep climb of around 175 metres taking around 30 minutes. At the top we meet a cobbled road leading right to **Pico Alto** and left to the park centre (Wp.17 163M).

Going left and passing the nursery on our right, we leave the cobbled road and follow a path behind **Casa da Ribeira das Cales** (Wp.18 171M) that leads through the woodland.

Casa da Ribeira das Cales

Soon crossing the tarred forest road, we then pick up a path through the gardens before crossing a bridge and climbing steps to reach the **Reception Centre** at **Ribeira das Cales** (Wp.19 180M).

.. beautifully planted ..

There's a wonderful variety of tree species here, including Cedars, Oaks and Laurels and the gardens and road verges around the two buildings are beautifully planted with many colourful endemic species including Pride of Madeira, chrysanthemum, Anemone-leaved Geranium, Black Parsley and Shrubby Sow Thistle.

In bygone days, **Monte** was an area preferred by English settlers due to its peaceful location and cooler climate, evidenced now by the legacy of colonial *quintas* and English gardens. Offering lots of variety and excitement, this trail from **Monte** to **Romeiros** starts in **Largo da Fonte**, passing beside palaces, gardens, churches and the toboggan run before ascending though lovely woodland with rocky crags, impressive waterfalls and spectacular deep valleys along the way. The charm of this historical trail is aptly described by the author Robert Goddard in his novel 'Past Caring', providing us with an opportunity to follow in the footsteps of his characters, as they make their way through a landscape of snowy blossoms and colourful flowers.

The route can be undertaken as a circular returning to **Monte**, our official trail, or as a linear walk to **Romeiros**. Alternatively, combine it with walks 8 & 9 to provide a continuous trail between the cultural settlements of **Monte** and **Camacha**, (15 kilometres) following **Levada dos Tornos**.

Due to both its links with the past and its close proximity to **Funchal**, this atmospheric trail is extremely popular, particularly with English tourists, but it does come at a price; some sections are unprotected, running alongside deep drops where the railings are damaged or in some places non-existent. If in doubt, turn back at the waterfall and follow the route in reverse to **Romeiros**.

Access by hire car or taxi: Follow the ER 103 from **Funchal** to **Monte**. The main car park is situated just above the village.

Access by public transport:
Town Buses N°s 20, 21 & 48 serve **Monte**. Alternatively take the *teleférico* for a spectacular ascent from **Funchal** seafront. Return from **Romeiros** on Town Bus N°29 to **Funchal**.

Starting out from the main square in **Monte** (Wp.1 0M), we head along **Caminho das Babosas** curving round the **Monte Palace Tropical Gardens** - there's the option of a visit to these beautiful gardens before we head off on the trail, or alternatively on return. Continuing along the cobbled lane, we walk between the Church of

Monte palace gardens

Senhora do Monte and the toboggan run, then pass the **Funchal/Monte** *teleférico*, before entering into **Babosas** square (Wp.2 7M).

The Jardim Botánico *teleférico*

The cobbled lane continues, descending steeply into the valley, soon passing the **Jardim Botánico** *teleférico*, before reaching a path junction (Wp.3 15M), signed 'Levada dos Tornos'. This is our return route, which emerges here following an ascent on the cobbled path through the forested slopes.

However, our outward trail runs along the valley wall, swinging left (17M) on an energetic uphill climb, getting steeper between the cliffs and the plunging valley before our final ascent to meet the **Levada dos Tornos** (Wp.4 31M) where it emerges from a tunnel.

The Levada dos Tornos tunnel

At around 1500 metres long, the tunnel starts in the southern area of the Ecological Park, the channel passing below **Terreiro da Luta** on its course east.

Ignoring this, we follow the *levada* downstream, immediately arriving at an impressive waterfall, where **Ribeira das Cales** plunges into the riverbed below (Wp.5).Now passing beneath the waterfall through a short tunnel, care is needed as we emerge to different scenery; the wooded slopes are replaced by sheer cliffs as we negotiate the eastern side of the **Ribeira de João Gomes** valley.

.. an impressive waterfall ..

Passing another waterfall, careful footwork is again needed along the next section until we reach a sluice gate on the channel (Wp.6 40M). From this position we have good views down to **Funchal** harbour . Another few minutes along we arrive at a cobbled path leading right from the *levada* (Wp.7 50M), our route back to **Babosas** square.

Those wishing to continue on to **Romeiros** or **Camacha** should continue

to follow the *levada* from this point. With more magnificent views down to **Funchal**, our route becomes less exposed due to increased undergrowth. Shortly we pass through a small hamlet where the channel is covered with slabs (Wp.11 55M); after another five minutes we arrive at a T-junction in **Romeiros** village where we leave the channel, turning right down steps to where the *levada* is signed in both directions (Wp.12 60M). Below the steps, a path leads down to the bus stop; those wishing to terminate the walk at this point can return to **Funchal** from here. Those wishing to continue on Walk 8 should continue from the signpost for around 15 metres, then go left up a short flight of steps to lead back onto the *levada*.

Our official circular route leaves the *levada* at the junction with the cobbled trail (Wp.7 50M), steadiy descending the eastern valley side amongst mimosa and eucalyptus on a steep zigzagged and stone-rippled section; we arrive at a junction with a path dropping down left (Wp.8 60M), another route to **Bom Successo** below the Botanical Gardens.

Our trail continues down, the gradient moderating before leading us over an impressive stone bridge (Wp.9 65M). From the tumbling waters of the **Ribeira João Gomes** we make an ascent up the western forested slopes, to emerge from the trees at the junction with our outward path to **Levada dos Tornos** (Wp.3 95M). Still climbing, we again pass the **Botánico Teleférico**, before a final steep ascent brings us up to **Babosas** square. Another five minutes walking and we are back in **Largo da Fonte** for a well-earned rest and refreshments (Wp.1 115M).

The broad path alongside **Levada dos Tornos**, which runs at around 600 metres and forms part of south-east Madeira's water system, is a popular walking route. This section is close to **Funchal** with easy access by bus, providing a mixture of old and new woodland, country houses and notable refreshment stops at either the **Horténsia Tea Rooms** or **Jasmin Tea House**.

This route forms the middle section between Walks 7 and 9 which combined, link the historic settlements of **Monte** and **Camacha**, meandering beside hedgerows of wild flora, abundant blossoms and cultivated gardens along its length.

Access by hire car or taxi: leave the VR1 at Junction 13 and follow the signs for the Botanical Gardens and the **Choupana Hills Hotel**. **Romeiros** village is situated around 1 km from the hotel.

Access by bus: take the **Funchal** Town Bus N°29 to **Romeiros**. Return from **Jasmin Tea House** on Town Bus N°47.

From the **Romeiros** bus stop, we take concrete steps and a cobbled path, going steeply up towards the village where we head to the signpost for 'Levada dos Tornos' (Wp.1 0M). Here we link with our Walk 7 at Wp.10. Fifteen metres along we take another short flight of steps on the left to reach the *levada*.

Crossing the water run-off (Wp.2)

Turning right, we pass through the settlement - rather frugal living here, so expect to be approached by locals selling flowers or offering directions - soon leaving the houses behind, we almost immediately reach a watercourse where we take steps up and back down onto the *levada* (Wp.2 5M).

The forest along most of the trail is predominantly pine, eucalyptus and three species of acacia - golden mimosa and silver and black wattle mimosa, their flowers ranging in colour from deep cream to vivid yellow; the acacias produce a mass of perfumed blossom during spring and early summer, often flowering again in early winter. The broad *levada* path is also lined with a profusion of wild flowers; many species of Fabaceae

(Pea) with lovely displays of Greater Periwinkle, (Vinca major), Red Flowering Sorrel (Oxalis purpurea), Red Valerian, Scarlet Pimpernel and the large white Calla Lilies (Calla aethiopica).

Greater Periwinkle

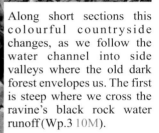

Along short sections this colourful countryside changes, as we follow the water channel into side valleys where the old dark forest envelopes us. The first is steep where we cross the ravine's black rock water runoff (Wp.3 10M).

Out of the valley, we turn into a second pocket of old forest, where we cross a hand railed bridge over a stream (Wp.4 15M) followed by a steel section of railings.

Emerging from the dark woodland, the old forest gives way to tall eucalyptus trees lending our route an airy feel as we stroll along above the **Romeiros** road with views down the valley. Passing caves in the cliff on

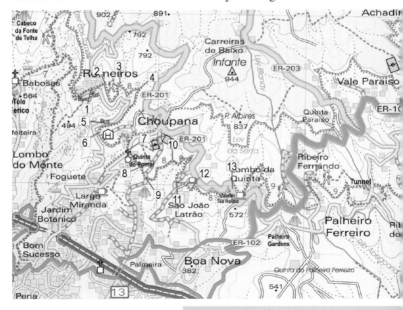

.. levada water house .. (Wp.8)

our left, we come to a section where the *levada* has been straightened and broad steps cross it above a bus stop on the road below us (Wp.5 22M). Curving left, this idyllic path is rudely interrupted as we reach a chain link gate, being the entrance to the **Choupana Hills Hotel** (Wp.6).

Crossing over the private road, we continue through the gardens along a 'public right of way' path, and after passing beside the hotel lodges, we leave the resort through a large wooden gate crossing the *levada*. Here a huge retaining wall appears on our left, behind which loom the hotel buildings.

Crossing over another road where the channel is tunnelled underneath, a sign appears indicatingthe direction to **Horténsia Tea Rooms** (Wp.7 34M). Continuing our stroll, we soon pass beside a *levada* water house and water change point beside a substantial circular water tank (Wp.8 38M), shortly before crossing a steep tarmac lane (Wp.9).

Passing a patch of houses (Wp.10 45M) which contrast with the meadow landscape, we now have good views over **Funchal**, as we cross over a road which bridges the channel (Wp.11 52M); a N°47 bus stop sits on the road above our route. Another couple of minutes along the agapanthus-lined path takes us over a concrete lane by the entrance to the **Horténsia Tea Rooms** (Wp.12 55M).

The **Horténsia**, in **Quinta Gorlick**, provide different seating areas within the exotic gardens, with gingham cloths and comfortable seating, from where we can sample the variety of the cakes and sandwiches on offer at our leisure.

Leaving **Horténsia**, we pass beside a circular water tank, and we suspect, a little pig farm; however this is not too much a blot on the landscape on this otherwise lovely route. Passing a large development, which appears to be relatively new but abandoned, we continue along another quiet stretch of forest through dappled sunlight and tunnels of mimosa blossom, before arriving a few minutes later at the ER 201 regional road (Wp.13 65M).

Our route ends at this point giving us the option to either retrace our steps back to **Romeiros**, to continue on the *levada* to link with Walk 9 or to return to **Funchal** on the N° 47 bus. For this final option turn right off the levada following the ER201 for around 300m down to the bus stop.

Another interesting walk along **Levada dos Tornos**, this trail forms the final section of our recommended continuous route between the settlements of **Monte** and **Camacha**. Passing through wooded slopes, the channel skirts rural areas where an abundance of wild flowers, spring blossoms and exotic gardens are found.

The trail passes close by **Quinta do Palheiro Ferreiro**, the estate of the famous English wine merchants, the Blandy family, offering the option of visiting these beautiful gardens. After leaving the estate, we negotiate a rather difficult tunnel, albeit with an optional detour. The final two kilometres (along the regional roads) ends in **Largo Conselheiro Aires de Ornelas**, the pretty square in the centre of **Camacha**.

O Relogio wicker factory and showroom

Camacha village is idyllically set on a plateau enveloped in woodland and, as well as being a good base for walkers, is famous for arts and crafts, basket making in particular; the village representing the centre of Madeira's willow craft industry.

Of a cultural nature, the village hosts the 'Apple Festival', a popular annual event, and is also home to one of the most famous Portuguese folklore groups 'Folclórico da Camacha', who have entertained throughout Europe and Internationally. Last but not least, the village has the honour of being the birthplace of Portuguese football; the country's first ever match was played here in 1895.

Access by hire car or taxi: leaving the **Via Rápida** at Junction 13, take the ER 102 signed 'Camacha'. **The Jasmin Tea House is** located 400 metres along the ER 201 regional road, signed 'Terreiro da Luta'. Roadside parking is available 200 metres above the tea rooms.

Access by bus: take the Town Bus N°47 to **Jasmin Tea House**, or access by extending our Walk 8 from **Romeiros**, bus N°29. Return to **Funchal** on N°77 from **Camacha**, N°s 110 and 114 from **Nogueira** or N°37 from **Palheiro Ferreiro**.

Picking up the **Levada dos Tornos** on the right of the road (Wp.1 0M), the channel first negotiates a newly excavated watercourse before passing along the tree-lined *levada* path. The first short section requires a little careful footwork but soon the path widens, taking us east along the waterway. It's an easy stroll along the flower lined channel as it contours round the hillside overlooking the main road settlements. After crossing the line of a watercourse, we pass below houses before meeting the top level of valley housing, and a path climbing up to a white house above the *levada*. With apple blossom and mimosa adorning our route, and views across to **Funchal** harbour, we soon meet and cross the regional ER-205 road (Wp.2 27M).

Back on the concrete *levada* path signed 'Levada dos Tornos, Camacha', **Palheiro Golf** is away on our right as we wind our way between houses and cultivated plots. As the water channel curves left, the *levada* goes underground by a large warehouse (Wp.3 30M), just after which, we emerge onto a tarmac road. Crossing over and passing in front of a couple of houses, the flower-bedecked *levada* continues before heading into the countryside.

Apple blossom along the *levada* shoulder

Tall eucalyptus soar skywards, constantly interspersed with houses, many with pretty gardens, before the channel swings right at a stream bed and water run-off point (Wp.4). Moving into deeper woodland, the trail becomes quieter and prettier with masses of wayside flowers before we reach the tunnel entrance (Wp.5 43M).

The shoulder through the tunnel (approx 300m long) is very narrow in places and low overhead, with slippery and wet sections underfoot making progress slow, but it is passable with care. Needless to say, a good torch is needed.

Alternative route

There is however a choice for an open air, overland, route. Following a right hand path at the entrance, we head through trees above the tunnel

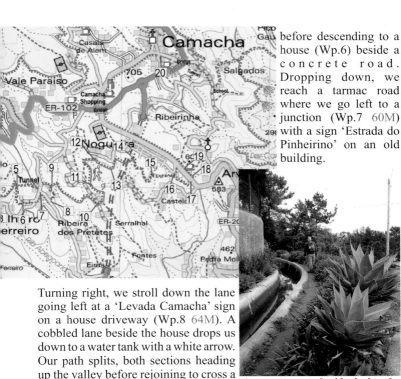

before descending to a house (Wp.6) beside a concrete road. Dropping down, we reach a tarmac road where we go left to a junction (Wp.7 60M) with a sign 'Estrada do Pinheirino' on an old building.

Turning right, we stroll down the lane going left at a 'Levada Camacha' sign on a house driveway (Wp.8 64M). A cobbled lane beside the house drops us down to a water tank with a white arrow. Our path splits, both sections heading up the valley before rejoining to cross a planked bridge (Wp.9 70M) to come onto the *levada*.

Agave attenuata beside the levada

Optional detour to visit Quinta do Palheiro Ferreiro gardens

On meeting the road junction at Wp.7, we can drop down right on the tarred road to bring us to the entrance to the gardens. The estate covers around 500 acres encompassing beautiful formal and wild gardens and natural woodland.

Back on the *levada*, we emerge from the tunnel (or from the alternative pathway), into a thin area of forest to eventually reach the **Rua do Pomar** road across from **Restaurant O Alentejana** (Wp.10 90M).

Crossing over, the *levada* curves below the restaurant to pass in front of affluent houses before bending left into a wooded valley where we have sight of the new VE5 **Camacha** road below us. Crossing a water run-off (Wp.11 94M) and swinging into a new valley, we stroll past a stream and an impressive stone stair leading to houses hidden among the trees (Wp.12 100M). Three minutes along, the *levada* runs between houses and a workshop (Wp.13 105M) with the option of leaving the waterway by stepping up onto a tarred road, the quickest route to **Camacha Shopping**. However, this choice not only misses out on the prettiest section of the *levada*, but heads through the not too pleasant area of the **Nogueira** housing estate, before joining the regional road. (This was necessary at one time due to closure of the channel at this point, but now reopened and

reinstated). We therefore recommend continuing along the *levada*). Passing beside houses with pretty gardens we arrive at a water house, where **Levada dos Tornos** disappears into a long tunnel (Wp.14 110M). (Impassable to walkers, it emerges in **Ribeirinha** below **Camacha** centre).

From this water change point, a narrow channel now branches off to the right, which we follow to pass through pleasant woodland with hedges of wild flowers and shrubs, as well as orange and lemon trees and many exotic plants along the way. Our narrow path becomes uneven, rocky and overgrown, mainly with gorse; long trousers and a long sleeved shirt are definitely recommended. Coming out of the natural woodland, with a rolling hill in front of us, we pass beside a high wall (Wp.15 115M) before bending right, the route now giving way to good views of the coast.

We soon reach a narrow concrete lane leading up to a terracotta tile factory with a cement chute (Wp.16 120M). We can leave the channel here to pass over the lane at the top, continuing along the tarred road beside the factory and, ignoring a left fork, our route follows the road round to the right bringing us down to **Bar O Pretinho** on the ER205 road. However, we decided to continue on the final section of *levada*, passing behind a small house before the channel disappears for a short distance beneath a lane; our path continues left up the banking to join the lane. (At the time of our survey, this short section had been obliterated by topsoil, but this presented no problem). On reaching the lane, we turn right for around ten metres picking up the channel again on our left (Wp.17 125M).

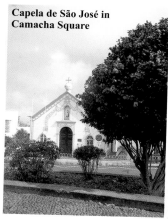

Capela de São José in Camacha Square

Continuing, we reach the ER205 where the water cascades down a chute to continue its flow down the roadside (Wp.18). **Bar O Pretinho** is located a few metres up the road on the left hand side (Wp.19 130M). From here we have a number of options; we can either take a bus or taxi into **Camacha** or back to **Funchal**, or walk into **Camacha** following the ER205. Climbing 100 metres over 1.2 kilometres brings us to **Camacha Shopping** and turning right here, it's another kilometre into the pretty square of **Largo Conselheiro Aires de Ornelas** in the centre of the village (Wp.20 185M).

This 'must do route' provides a wonderful contrast to forest or *levada* walking; breathtaking scenery and wild landscape with amazing rock formations, rugged cliffs and coves carved out by the sea; it's an unforgettable experience.

.. amazing rock formations ..

The rock formations along the entire route are truly amazing, with basalt veins or dykes running down through the multi-coloured layers of volcanic rock. A protected area within the **Parque Natural da Madeira,** the peninsula is quite arid due to its low hills and exposure to the north winds.

Signs request that we keep to the official paths and diversions to avoid erosion and enable recovery of important areas of flora. 138 species of plants have been identified on the peninsula, of which 31 are endemic to Madeira. Along sections of the route during spring and summer we can find carpets of Madeira Sea Stock (Matthiola maderensis), Madeira Marigolds (Calendula maderensis) and Mandon's Chrysanthemum (Argyranthemum pinnatifidum), Everlasting Flower (Helichrysum devium) and Pride of Madeira (Echium Nervosum).

Matthiola and Argyranthemum plants flourish here

.. the rare ice Plant ..

Other abundant species include Purple Viper's Bugloss (Echium plantagineum) and the rare Ice Plant (Mesembryanthemum crystallinum) found only on **São Lourenço**, its small white icy flower heads with green and red basal leaves.

In former times it was cultivated for its soda content and used in soap production.

Bird-watchers are likely to see the Berthelot's Pipit, Goldfinch, the Common Canary and Kestrels as well as protected marine birds such as Cory's Shearwater, Storm-Petrel and the Common Tern.

This understandably popular though fairly strenuous trail can be undertaken any time of year, though it's best to choose a clear day when the entire landscape is enhanced by sparkling sea and blue sky. The path zigzags from south to north, taking in views of the magnificent coastline. In places we find ourselves clambering over rocky ridges where the path can often become vague, although cairns and way marks keep us on track. On other sections we follow rocky mule tracks as well as crossing over a spectacular land bridge.

All dangerous sections are protected and wooden decking has been laid on some sections of pathway to avoid erosion.

Access by car: follow the VR1 to **Caniçal** and continue on the ER-109 to the car park at **Baia d'Abra**.

Access by bus: S.A.M. bus N°113 **Funchal - Caniçal**.

We start out from the car park at the end of the ER-109 (Wp.1 0M) from where a well-trodden path drops down into the valley and here, looking across the **Baia d'Abra**, we can see a circular rock arch over the sea, above which is a small mountain. This lies beyond **Casa do Sardinha**, our destination. Leaving the valley floor (Wp.2), we follow the newly-laid wooden decking to climb up the northern side of the valley with the **Pedras Brancas** trig point above us on the left.

.. an amazing 30-metre high rock tower rises up ..

Our route levels out to run along to a stone wall and a signboard (Wp.3 10M) before twin paths take us past the next white post (Wp.4) to curve around the hillside where we meet a crossroads (Wp.5 16M). On the left is a cliff-edge *miradouro* over the rocky north coast bay of **Pedra Furada**, where an amazing 30-metre high rock tower rises up out of the sea. The right hand path leads down to a pebble beach on the **Baía d'Abra** but our route continues ahead.

We soon start to climb over a rocky area to reach a white post (Wp.6); more posts and cairns guide us (Wp.7 23M) as we climb to a crest (Wp.8) followed by a short descent (Wp.9) before contouring round to a second

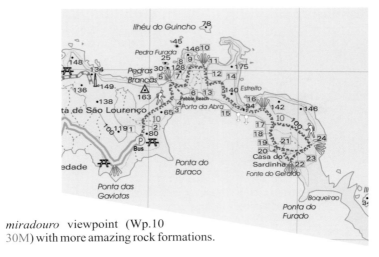

miradouro viewpoint (Wp.10 30M) with more amazing rock formations.

From here the path runs across a saddle to a junction (Wp.11) with another *miradouro* viewpoint a few metres to our left, and then undulates along, climbing gently to come under a mass of weathered rock, a natural rock fence crossing our path (Wp.12) as it runs down into the valley.

Coming to the end of the rock section (Wp.13), we swing left into a gentler grassed valley, crossing its dry watercourse (Wp.14 40M) before turning out of the valley to come above the cliffs and fish farms.

The natural rock bridge

A gentle climb brings us up to the stone marker on the summit of the ridge (Wp.15 45M), its northern side plunging down to the ocean. We descend to a natural land bridge, the narrowest point on the peninsula with 100-metre drops on either side down to the sea.

Sturdy steel posts linked by steel hawsers give us safe guidance across this previously difficult **Estreito** section, which looks trickier from the top of the ridge than it is when we actually pick our way down over the rock.

From here we have excellent views of the lighthouse on **Ilhéu do Farol**, a separate islet at the far end of the peninsula. Also in view are the **Ilhas das Desertas** further out to sea and on a clear day, good views of **Porto Santo** to the north east (Wp.16 56M). From the land bridge it's then a short distance before **Casa do Sardinha** comes into view.

Casa do Sardinha

This small single-storey building with a terracotta tiled roof was once a private dwelling reached by boat at the nearby jetty. The house, now base for a group of rangers, is surrounded by a small garden with giant Date Palms, Cycads and Tamarisk trees, a green oasis in this dry grassy landscape and rocky terrain.

Arriving at a junction (Wp.17), we have a choice of a clockwise or an anti-clockwise tour encircling the house. We go down to the right (anti-clockwise), looking back to take in the impressive views of the undercut cliffs below the land bridge. As we descend we pass a marker post (Wp.18) guiding us down to a junction (Wp.19 65M) to overlook the tiny quay (Wp.20), where steps lead down to the sea for optional bathing.

Turning away from the quay, we take the path up towards the house, a lovely place for a rest and picnic, before going right at a junction beyond the garden (Wp.21), to reach a cliff-top viewpoint (Wp.22). Continuing to curve above **Casa do Sardinha**, (Wp.23 80M) we pass another viewpoint on the right (Wp.24) before arriving back at the junction with our outward route (Wp.17) and returning from here to our start point.

The view from Pico do Facho

The first place on the island to be colonized and Madeira's capital during the first century of occupation, **Machico** is built around a lovely natural bay and, although relatively small, it now has a new marina and an attractive waterfront with sandy beaches, as well as a bustling centre with shops, bars and restaurants.

The Parochial Church of **Machico**, dedicated to Nossa Senhora da Conceição, is found in the main square framed by huge plane trees; it's well worth a visit. Our trail however, starts at the **Caniçal** tunnel leading us first to **Pico do Facho** (323 metres), which not only offers superb views over Madeira's east coast, the **São Lourenço** peninsula and the **Ilhas Desertas** but also provides a fantastic vantage point over **Funchal** airport; the aircraft seem close enough to pluck out of the sky as they make their landing approach to the runway. The final section of the route leads us down a donkey trail to end in the centre of the town.

Access by hire car or taxi: from **Machico**, follow the ER109 regional road towards **Caniçal**, parking at the entrance to **Túnel do Caniçal**.

Access by bus: take the Nº113 Machico-Caniçal bus.

From the entrance to the **Túnel do Caniçal** (Wp.1 0M), we set off up the **Pico do Facho** road. It's an energetic, steady ascent, rewarded by increasing panoramas over the **Machico** valley as we climb past the green gates of a water treatment site to the right, and a little further along and to our left, a cottage

MACHICO

with its own fire engine.

We soon reach the point where the old **Machico-Caniçal** donkey trail crosses the road (Wp.2 18M), some fifteen metres before an electricity pylon, then continue to slog up the last few metres of the tarmac road, with views now opening up over **Caniçal** (Wp.3), before we turn right and come up to the parking area below **Pico do Facho**. Pathways take us up the slopes below the transmitter to find a suitable vantage point (Wp.4 23M).

Descending to the donkey trail at Wp.2

When we are sated with the views, we head back down the road - far easier down than up, of course - until we again reach the donkey trail (Wp.2 30M). Turning left, we start to drop down the rough boulder path, often hidden by long grass, to come alongside a stone wall.

Our path divides (Wp.5 38M) and we go right and down across the sloping meadow, the path now more stone than grass. Coming below a small rock outcrop (Wp.6 50M), we go left. Our route, at times a narrow river of rubble, angles down across the meadow, and then curves right to drop towards a residential home which has cut the old trail, where we have to go left alongside the fencing to drop down onto a 'new' road (Wp.7 56M).

Once in front of the impressive building Casa da Misericórdia e Grace, roughly translating to 'Home of Mercy & Grace', we have two descent options. From here, we can drop steeply down **Caminho da Quinta Palmeira**, turning left onto **Rua da Banda de Além**; however, our route goes left here along the 'new' **Estrada de Misericórdia** road, for a gentler but longer descent.

Machico Marina

It's an easy walk above houses before we drop down to meet the new marina (Wp.8) where we go right along the promenade and into **Banda de Além** square by the bridge (Wp.9 76M), where we are close to a choice of bar/restaurants for refreshments.

Few people realise that the **Levada do Caniçal** continues beyond the road tunnel; whilst the start beneath a quarry is unimpressive, the main part of our route passes through beautiful countryside and woodland which has escaped the depredations of the area's expansion and new highway.

Caniçal, a parish of **Machico** situated 20 kilometres north-east of **Funchal**, is now an important area accommodating the island's new industrial port: agriculture and fishing being originally its main industry. Our trail, along a vast escarpment, circles the northern boundary of the town and en-route provides stunning views of the coastline to the **São Lourenço** peninsula with the **Desertas** islands also in view to the south.

Access by hire car or taxi: from **Machico**, follow the ER109 regional road towards **Caniçal**. The walk begins on the eastern side of **Túnel do Caniçal** where parking is available in a lay-by alongside a quarry and maintenance depot, a few metres from the tunnel entrance.

Access by bus: N°113 **Machico-Caniçal** route.

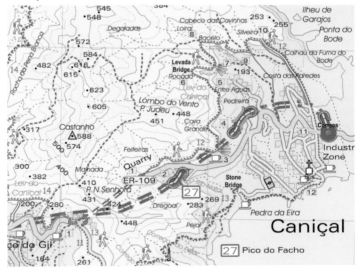

Stairs at the eastern end of the road tunnel lead up to a shrine, worthy of a quick peep, whilst at the bottom of the steps (Wp.1 0M), the **Levada do Caniçal** leaves the road on the left to traverse a handrail section and negotiate a narrow unprotected drop. We can either follow the channel from this point, or pick up the *levada* at the top of the quarry access road (Wp.2 5M), thus avoiding the first short section, signed "danger of falling rocks".

Our path runs along a boulder wall before we tackle another unprotected drop where the *levada* and path clings to a cliff face. Initially there's quite a lot of noise from the quarry, but soon we leave its boundaries behind, to pass below the craggy escarpment and take in our first views of the coastline. Rounding a bluff (Wp.3 17M), the path improves as we head north across grassy slopes into the **Cova Grande** valley. Passing beside a water change point (20M), the *levada* is piped for a short section until we reach the valley head when it reverts to running water.

On approaching the uppermost houses of **Caniçal** we have fine views from our elevated position over the **São Lourenço** peninsula; we lingered on a rocky spot beneath a solitary Cypress tree (Wp.4 26M) to take in the views and to watch the spectacular aerobatics of a male Kestrel lower down the escarpment.

The hillside becomes steeper and wilder as we curve into another valley; ahead are huts and cultivated terraces served by a dirt road that climbs up the valley and replaces the *levada* path (Wp.5 30M).

The views from Wp.4

Below a large hut, we leave the dirt road on the right, to follow the water channel before swinging left into a tree-filled valley. As we stroll through the acacia woodland, the path and channel become quite overgrown; on reaching a small *levada* bridge over the valley's watercourse (Wp.6 37M) we must wade across the short muddy channel to reach the opposite bank; but in this beautiful woodland, it's no hardship to take a few minutes 'drying out' after the crossing.

From the bridge, we stroll through the flower-filled woodland to come out of the trees to views over the peninsula (Wp.7 41M), our route now curving through more open woodland into another valley. Across the valley floor, the *levada* heads out to pass the remains of huts and terraces before crossing a water runoff bridged over the watercourse.

A Red Admiral

We swing into another tree-filled valley, now with eucalyptus appearing, the water channel edged with a riot of flowers enhanced by the frequent appearance of Red Admiral and Monarch butterflies. Across the valley's watercourse and a dirt track (Wp.8), plants almost overwhelm the channel, requiring careful footwork to avoid stepping into the water.

All too soon this floriferous valley changes to open woodland; a small culvert taking water down the hillside on our right (Wp.9 58M) shortly before the *levada* swings right to run downhill beside a wide forest track (Wp.10 62M).

.. spectacular views of the north side of the peninsula ..

Our final stage is an easy stroll down the earthen road where we enjoy spectacular views of the north side of the peninsula and of the impressive red dry creeks lying below the forested slopes to the west. On reaching a domed water reservoir with the industrial zone fence on our left, the track becomes a tarmac lane heading down past the first houses, where we come onto a junction beside the *correios* (post office) (Wp.11 80M) with the 'end of motorway' roundabout on our left.

Straight over the junction, we follow **Estrada da Banda d'Além** down towards the new church before the street swings right to come into the centre of **Caniçal** by its old chapel, bus stop, taxis and some well-earned refreshments at **Bar Moreira** (Wp.12 84M), a bar so laid back, it's almost supine.

This route can be combined with Walk 13 - The Old Trail to Caniçal (following it in reverse) to make a circular walk back to **Túnel do Caniçal** or alternatively as a linear route by combining with Walk 13 (in reverse), and Walk 12 along the donkey trail, to return to **Machico** centre.

There was a time before the ER-109 road when the main access to **Caniçal** was by donkey trail over the **Facho** ridge. When considered from standing in **Machico** it looks a daunting prospect, but with a little effort you can enjoy the wild landscapes between these two towns; our 'main route', starting from the **Caniçal** Tunnel entrance will however save you a considerable climb.

The old coastal path is now little walked and even less maintained; a shame, as it takes us through delightful countryside providing a refreshing change to forest and *levada* walking. Although rather rocky underfoot and overgrown in places, the route is quite discernable and easy to follow with the help of red markings and there are no precipitous sections.

Access by hire car or taxi: follow directions for Walks 11 & 14.

Access by bus: N°113 bus to **Túnel do Caniçal** entrance. Return on the N°113 bus from **Caniçal**.

Alternative start from Machico: Follow directions (in reverse) for Walk 11 - Pico do Facho - Machico (Wp's 9 - 2). Add 1 walker, 1 hour and 280 metres of ascent.

Official start from Túnel do Caniçal
Alighting from the N°113 bus at the start of the **Pico do Facho** road (Wp.1 0M), we stride up the tarmac leaving the houses behind, the gradient steepening to bring us to a water treatment station on our right, then passing below a cottage with a fire tender in its drive. After a 'croaking frog pond' in an old quarry, we continue to ascend again to meet the 'old coastal path', which crosses the road by a pylon (Wp.2 18M).

It's quite a slog up the road, but we recommend continuing the climb as far as the picnic area at **Pico do Facho** (refer to Walk 11), to enjoy the views

down over **Machico** and the magnificent coastline along to the **São Lourenço** peninsula. Add around 20 minutes for this diversion as walk timings are for continuous walking from Wp.2.

Our track now gently descends northeast as it curves around the hillside to a junction. Ignoring a track off to the right, we curve north as the track narrows to a path above the steep **Corrego do Ilhéu** valley. The path drops down quite steeply before levelling out below traditional huts, then crossing the bowl of the valley above the steep cleft down to the sea.

.. an excellent if windy viewpoint ..

Ahead, a pylon surmounts a bare ridge and the trail starts climbing gently through tree-dotted slopes towards it, getting narrower and steeper as we push through tall heather to come onto the promontory beside the pylon (Wp.3 42M), an excellent if windy viewpoint over the rugged coastal landscape.

The path now has a discontinuity on the bare rock and it's easy to think the onward route is down the line of the ridge, but no! Facing the pylon, our correct route is left and behind us dropping down along the northern side of the ridge. Our narrow, eroded path drops through mimosa trees to emerge between long abandoned terraces as we cross the valley's watercourse (Wp.4 49M). Stone walls guide us round a rocky ridge into a smaller, steeper valley notable for its rock walls. Our path narrows before turning northeast towards **Caniçal** . When the route divides at a sheet of rock (with an old red paint waymark) we stay on the upper path for a gentle ascent along the top of a boulder wall.

Pride of Madeira

Coming alongside a rock outcrop the peninsula again comes into view; on rounding the outcrop we're looking down on **Caniçal** (Wp.5 74M). Our path runs inland below the outcrop before descending in zigzags, the route again confirmed by old red waymarks.

The vegetation along the whole of this trail is typical of the island's coastal areas with Pride of Madeira , Prickly Pear and Globe Flower particularly dominant.

Over a stone ridge, our path now runs inland across grassy slopes to round a cleft slashed into the hillside before continuing down past old walls, coming high above the pebble beach at the mouth of the **Ribeira Natal** valley where the stone bridge comes into view (Wp.6 93M); if walking the route in reverse make sure you keep

Prickly Pear

right at this point as continuing straight ahead leads to an impressive dead-end at the top of the cliffs.

Our path becomes rockier, requiring concentration, as we drop towards the valley floor. A steep, scrambling descent finally brings us down to the stone bridge over the watercourse (Wp.7 103M).

The stone bridge at Wp.7

Another few metres along, we meet a tarmac road serving the beach, where we turn right to stroll down to the mini yacht club and bar (Wp.8 106M). After refreshment (optional but recommended), we pass along the new but rather neglected beach-front promenade, which leads us to Caniçal's road system (Wp.9). The new Whale Museum, the **Museu da Baleira**, a very impressive stone building, now stands on the corner at this junction and is due to open its doors to the public in October 2009.

.. the lovely restored chapel ..

From the museum our trail takes us along the seafront passing beside the swimming pool as we head towards the harbour. Taking a left turn on **Rua da Calão**, running between a restaurant on the right and a garden area on the left where local men appear to spend the day playing cards under large palm trees, we have only a short climb to bring us into **Caniçal** square beside the lovely restored chapel and where **Bar Moreira** is conveniently situated alongside the bus stop and taxis (Wp.10 121M).

The popular 'Dangerous Gateway', **Boca do Risco** offers fine views along Madeira's rugged north coast. As we stand on the cliff tops, waves crash below us, while on clear days we can pick out **Porto Santo** to the north-east.

This is a section of a longer walking trail, for centuries the shortest route between **Machico** and **Porto Cruz**. However, the northern coastal path beyond **Boca do Risco** runs along a vertiginous cliff face as it makes its steep descent through the agricultural settlement of **Larano** before arriving in **Porto da Cruz**. If you wish to walk this further route, we suggest joining a guided group; even the most experienced mountain walkers should only attempt it in good weather and not forget this quote from a previous walker " .. the most dangerous and vertiginous path we used all week."

The first part of our trail is along **Levada do Caniçal**, then on a narrow path which climbs through farmland and woodland to finally reach the saddle of **Boca do Risco**. The pathway up to **Boca** is straightforward, although can become quite slippery in wet weather so, heeding the advice given above, we also recommend this shortened route in dry weather only.

Access by hire car or taxi: from **Machico**, follow the ER109 regional road towards **Caniçal**, parking at the entrance to **Túnel do Caniçal**.

Access by bus: N°113 to **Túnel do Caniçal**. Return N°113 from **Ribeira Seca**.

We start from the **Caniçal** tunnel entrance, crossing the road to a pretty little water house beside the *levada* (Wp.1 0M).

.. a pretty little water house ..

Following the channel north-west and passing beside houses above the **Caniçal** road, we take around 45 minutes to negotiate this section of the *levada* as it winds in and out of small side valleys, crosses streams and passes through stands of acacia and eucalyptus.

It's a gentle rural area of agricultural terraces; sugar cane, banana and vines abound. Along most of the route we enjoy panoramic views of the

The weekender hut at Wp.2

vast **Machico** valley. Passing small farm sheds and one cute and colourful 'weekender' hut (Wp.2 25M), clearly cherished by its owner with an amusing garden character working the water pump, we now leave the main valley and after passing steps leading up to a large hut (Wp.3 35M), we eventually reach our **Boca** trail where a narrow path comes up from the hamlet below, to cross diagonally over the water channel. (Wp.4 45M)*

The Machico valley

However, our destination is the crest on the northern cliffs, so from the junction, signed 'Vereda da Boca do Risco', we now follow the path right on a stone-laid trail which climbs steadily past a hut and terraces, going through a grove of mimosas before curving above more cultivated areas and huts (Wp.5).

Our path is a narrow brown ribbon which contours above the plots before curving into a sharp cleft in the valley wall. Crossing a watercourse (Wp.6 57M), it then runs over rocks before curving back to wind through the tall pines which line the main valley. Swinging right into another pine-filled pocket with the beautiful wild hillside above us, we cross another watercourse (Wp.7) to climb above the trees where we then sweep back into the main valley. In this wild, natural landscape, it's a surprise to come across a smallholding (Wp.8 68M) where 'Boca do Risco' is signed left along a narrow dirt path; careful footwork is now required through intrusive vegetation.

Soon, though, we are back to heading north on a good path for the long, steady climb up to the natural gate in the cliff top ridge that is **Boca do Risco** (Wp.9 75M). We pass through the **Boca**, and just beyond it, are rewarded with spectacular views along Madeira's northern coastline.

.. spectacular views ..

Lingering for a while in this idyllic location, and perhaps having a picnic, we then return along the same path, again with careful footwork on the narrow sections, before re-joining the **Levada do Caniçal** (Wp.4 98M). Crossing over the channel, our return route now takes us down the traditional path for a steady descent into a valley scattered with cottages, farms and newer properties.

The rough path soon becomes concrete (Wp.10 104M) and gains street lights as we head down to the village of **Ribeira Seca** where a short flight of steps eventually leads us onto a tarred road (Wp.11 110M). Heading south, we soon reach **Bar Boca do Risco** (Wp.12 112M) before continuing through the village to end our walk on the ER109 regional road (Wp.13 120M), where the bus stop can be found nearby.

As an alternative to taking a taxi or public transport, this route can be extended by walking to and from the start and finish points, either by following the ER109, or alternatively following a quieter street passing through **Banda da Além** square, which lies across the bridge from **Machico**'s main square. Add around 70 metres in ascents and descents for this option.

Penha d'Águia

Portela is the starting point for this wonderful forest walk through the best area of *laurisilva* on the south side of the island. The walk begins at the viewpoint offering views north to **Porto da Cruz** and **Faial**, the huge rock mass of **Penha d'Águia** dominating the scene.

Our destination is the hamlet of **Maroços** in the municipality of **Machico**, a small community untouched by tourism where we are guaranteed a warm and friendly reception .

The trail is suitable for most abilities and intersects with one of the official (PBTT JOEL) routes, designated suitable for disabled people using adapted wheelchairs, as well as for cyclists. The Joel route is well signed and field coded throughout, but the walking route (PR5) is not, therefore it is necessary to follow the older, rustic signs 'Vereda das Funduras - Percurso Pedonal', until we reach the Environmental Education Centre in the **Funduras** forest.

3 | 3H 40M | 8.7 km | neg 420m | | 2

Access by hire car or taxi: follow the VR1 to **Machico** then take the VE1 signed 'Santana and Porto da Cruz'. At the end of the third tunnel, turn left following the signposts for 'Portela'. The viewpoint is located a few kilometers along the narrow secondary road.

Access by bus: S.A.M: Bus N°156 serves **Maroços** for the outward journey to **Funchal**. Alternatively N°s 23 and 113 run between **Machico** and **Funchal** and **Ribeira Seca** and **Funchal** respectively.

Leaving the (PR5) information board at the viewing platform and walking beside the **Miradouro da Portela Bar/Restaurant** (Wp.1 0M) we follow the tarred lane, passing a number of pretty flower stalls before the road swings right and we turn left onto a wide dirt road signed 'Portela'. Our route is now lined with tall pines and cedars with a tiny *levada* flowing on our right; as the road bends to the right we arrive at another viewpoint, again overlooking the north coast (Wp.2 10M)

Continuing, we pass a number of irrigation tunnels bored through the hillside before meeting with a junction where we keep left (Wp.3 20M); the right hand path climbs up the hillside to a transmitter station.

Entering the forest, Wp.4

Now gently strolling along the track, we arrive at a 'Serra das Funduras' sign on our right (Wp.4 25M) where we enter into the forest. The forest floor is spongy under our feet and whilst pines still abound, the natural vegetation soon takes over.

With the trail undulating and gaps appearing through the trees, we get our first glimpse of the **Desertas Islands** and of the **Santo da Serra Golf** course to the southwest. This first section of forest negotiates a number of valley heads and small gorges before reaching a short flight of steps where we rejoin the wide dirt road (Wp.5 67M). Turning right and descending for a few metres, we then arrive at a picnic site on our left.

The dirt road bends to the right from here, but we leave it to climb up through the picnic site, passing another older signboard (Wp.6 70M) before veering right into the forest. From this point we have views of the forest road as it continues to snake down the hillside, with a second left hand track climbing to a forestry house (the Environmental Education Centre) set in the trees which our forest trail heads for. The forest maintenance roads are used for the 'Joelette' disabled and cycle trail, offering a reasonably even terrain as they wind across the hillside, eventually leading to **Fajã dos Rolos** above **Machico**.

... it's extremely green ..

The sub-tropical *laurisilva* forest along these two sections is quite beautiful if damp and humid; it's extremely green thanks to the magnificent displays of European Chain Fern and Lady Fern which appear to have taken over, many of these growing to tree proportions.

At the time of our survey, we also found fascinating clumps of fungi including Oyster mushrooms (Pleurotus sp.), large red and white toadstools (Amanita muscaria) and Lauribasidium Lauri Fungi, the latter only found on Bay Laurels (Laurus Azorica) in Madeira, the Canaries and the Azores.

As the forest thins and large pines start to appear we reach a short stairway, which we descend to arrive at **Casa das Funduras** (Wp.7 110M). The education centre is surrounded by natural gardens from where there are good views of the south coast. Ascending the track in front of the house we can make a 700 metre detour to **Miradouro do Larano**

(Wp.8 130M) to look down over **Pico do Facho** and **Machico**. Following lunch and a break at either the *miradouro* or the education centre, it's time to decide on our return options.

Our route follows the official (PR5) trail to end in **Maroços**, providing a

Casa das Funduras

contrast in terrain and landscape which happens to be the quickest route back to civilization and only 1.7 km down to the village. Other options include returning by the same route back to our starting point, or alternatively following the forest maintenance roads, either back to **Portela**, or descending to **Fajã dos Rolos** (a distance of 4.7 kilometres) ending at **Bar O Caniçal** from where we can arrange for a taxi to take us back to **Portela** or **Machico**. Returning along either of the forest roads will take around two hours and in our opinion, these are not particularly pleasant walking routes.

However, back on the official trail, we leave the education centre and the indigenous forest behind us, and walk 200 metres down the access road to reach a junction with another forest road (Wp.9 147M) signed 'Portela' right and 'Fajã dos Rolos' left. At the time we researched this walk there were no route markings for the (PR5) walking trail so careful attention to this route description is essential.

Going left at the junction, we descend to a second junction with a track going off left (Wp.10 152M). We ignore this and continue straight on to a second left hand junction (Wp.11 157M). Looking left, we see a red and yellow 'X' field code sign warning that the left turn is the 'wrong route'; however this relates only to the disabled/cycling route and not to our walking trail. Left is our route to **Maroços**.

And so, descending left at this T-junction, we follow the forest track, which leads us through pine and eucalyptus woodland. Dropping quite steeply on a slippery surface, it then swings right alongside a deep valley on our left. A few minutes later we encounter another left hand track leading into the valley (Wp.12 167M). Ignoring this, we continue for two minutes to a junction with a right hand grassy track, which is our route (Wp.13 169M).

Two minutes from the junction, our track veers left (Wp.14 171M). The path sweeps down the hillside and soon we pass beside small A-framed farm buildings with red tin roofs scattered around the agricultural plots. In places the path is uneven and also muddy in wet weather, so care is needed on this descent. As the track ends, we pick up a steep stone stairway dropping down between the rural house with their lovely flower gardens (Wp.15 183M).

The views across the hillside are magnificent, agricultural terraces sweeping down to the settlements below; looking across to our right, we can now make out the forest ridge leading to **Fajã dos Rolos**.

Steeply descending beside more houses, farm buildings and cultivated plots, we cross over **Levada do Caniçal** (Wp.16 213M), where we meet a concrete drive dropping and turning left to become a tarred road.

Going straight ahead on **Caminho do Lombo Raçada**, we continue to descend the steps and pathway between the houses. After a short and steep zigzag descent, we reach the village road beside the river where we cross the bridge to the centre of **Maroços** (Wp.17 220M).

Bus N°156 leaves from the centre close to this point; alternatively we can arrange for a taxi to collect us (the local driver Fernando can be contacted on 91 78 40 983 - the transfer back to **Portela** will cost around 10€). Otherwise call into one of the village bars and they will call a taxi to any location.

The **Ribeira de São Roque** valley rises from the foot of **Penha d'Águia** and extends to the forested slopes below **Ribeiro Frio**, with **Pico das Torres** and **Pico Ruivo** dominating the western vistas.

Levada do Castelejo leads us through this mountainous landscape, adorned with lush vegetation, before transcending into the *laurisilva*, eventually bringing us to the source of *levada* beside the picturesque pools and waterfalls of the **São Roque** river bed. This is a relatively easy walk along a comfortable path, but you should be sure-footed and have a good head for heights to negotiate a number of quite precipitous sections, which are mostly fenced but on our last survey these were broken in some places, offering no protection.

Access by car: follow the narrow road up from **Cruz** village, signed 'Levada do Castelejo'. Keeping right at a junction, the lane crosses the channel just before the tarmac ends; there is adequate parking above or below the waterway.

Access by bus: bus routes 53 and 78 serve **Cruz** and **Referta** villages.

The hamlet of **Cruz**, lying on a mountain ridge between **Porto da Cruz** and **Faial**, is the starting point for this lovely walk, heading westwards from the road junction (Wp.1 0M). First passing alongside agricultural terraces and vineyards, our trail sweeps left to wind its way into the **São Roque** valley. At this point we look across at the picturesque village of **São Roque do Faial** set against a backdrop of mountains, with **Penha d'Águia** (Eagle Rock) and the north coast to our right.

Taking care along this first section, flimsy fencing soon

Alternative (1¼ hours each way)
For those not wishing to tackle the main route - though if you can cope with the drops we definitely recommend it - an alternative is to follow the *levada* eastwards from **Cruz** village to **Referta**. Nature changes and the channel becomes a quiet blue ribbon contouring around the northern slopes and passing through a region of rural tranquility. Looking down on cultivated plots and small settlements, we enjoy excellent flora with mimosas, pines and young oaks prominent along this section of the channel

The trail eventually curves right into the large valley above **Ribeira Tem-te Não Caias**, (which loosely translates as 'Take care not to fall' river) before arriving at a *miradouro* viewpoint over the valley. A little later we enter a short and relatively comfortable tunnel; this can be avoided by following an energetic stair ascent and descent.

Once out of the tunnel, the *levada* curves right below houses to come below the bus stop in upper **Referta**, where steps take us up onto the 'main' road by the **Cruz da Garda** junction.

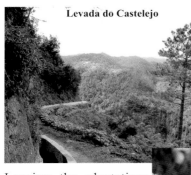
Levada do Castelejo

appears (Wp.2 10M) as we progress along the muddy shoulder. Here the valley is deep; on the opposite side, the **Levada de Baixo** is clearly visible, as is the high waterfall of **Água d'Alto**, crashing over the valley side into the **São Roque** river (Wp.3 16M).

Leaving the plantations behind, we wind our way alongside rocky walls before the channel again swings left passing beneath overhanging rock (Wp.4 24M). With stunning views

Sweet Violets

Rock navelwort

all the way and the sound of the river filling the air, we transcend into the natural forest where carpets of flowers adorn our route. White Eupatorium and many species of the pea family (Fabaceae) predominate, but interspersed with these, we can find Greater Periwinkle (Vinca major), Three-Cornered Leek (Allium triquetrum), Red Flowering Sorrel (Oxalis purpurea), Violets, Scarlet Pimpernel and the large white Calla Lilies (Calla aethiopica).

Passing another unprotected section where the path is also eroded, we soon reach a valley head (Wp5 38M); here a stream trickles over the *levada* before dropping into the valley below, the ideal habitat for a rich variety of ferns, mosses and lichens. Of particular interest is the bright green Navelwort growing from the rocky crevices; its fleshy basal leaves resemble the human navel, hence its name (Umbilicus rupestris), producing long stalks with white and green tubular spring flowers.

As we head into a deep gorge we cross a water run-off where the *levada* diverts into a stream (Wp.6 54M) before flowing on to contour more valley heads with sections of path which require care. Now approaching the main valley with the mountains and forested slopes above us, the **São Roque** river becomes loud and visible as we look down on pretty pools below (Wp.7 69M).

Another fifteen minutes and we arrive at the source of the irrigation channel where the shoulder ceases and we must drop down a few steps to the riverbed where the water tumbles over huge boulders forming pools in the rock.

As we progress a little further, climbing over the rocks, we arrive at a weir and an amazingly clear pool in the rocky bed (Wp.8 85M), an ideal spot to stop for rest and refreshments. It's also possible to wander a little further up the river on a vague left-hand path, bringing us to a

The weir at the *levada*'s source

Views to São Roque and Faial

number of rushing waterfalls, where we can further enjoy the tranquility and beauty of this location.

Our return to the starting point (Wp.1 170M) is by the same route, but now the perspective changes, giving

us lovely views of the north coastal villages dominated by the rocky promontory of **Eagle Rock**.

Arco de São Jorge, the most westerly parish of **Santana**, and **Boa Ventura**, a parish of **São Vicente**, lie in a lush forested area of the north coast, the latter nestling at the northern edge of the **Ribeira Porco** valley, spreading down from the central mountain range. **Boa Ventura** is a small agricultural village clustered around the church, which stands on a cobbled terrace overlooking the village and the mountains. The ER101 connects these two small communities, twisting and climbing for 5.5 kilometres and passing through two tunnels en-route. Prior to their construction in the 1950s, access between these two communities was only possible along the **Caminho da Entrosa** path, which is cut into the sea cliffs. This is the route we follow on this stunning walk, which rewards us with superb views along the coastline, wonderful natural vegetation and interesting rock formations.

This walk can be approached either from **Arco de São Jorge** or in the opposite direction from **Boa Ventura** so could be done there-and-back or one way, using taxi or bus to link start and finishing points.

Access by hire car or taxi: from the west, approach via **Ribeira Brava** and **São Vicente** taking the ER101 east to the village of **Arco de São Jorge** (14.5 km). From the east, approach via **Santana** on the VE1 continuing west on the ER101 to **Arco de São Jorge**. The walk starts at **Restaurante O Arco** situated on the coastal side of the road, west of the village.

Access by bus: Rodoeste Bus N°6 **Funchal - Boaventura** and **Arco de São Jorge**, via **São Vicente**. Horário Bus - N°103 **Funchal - Arc de São Jorge**, via **Santana**.

The old trail begins at **Restaurante O Arco** (Wp.1 0M) following a cobbled path which initially runs alongside agricultural plots and small garden orchards, lined a little further along with Australian Cheesewood; an introduced species which produces fragrant flowers in spring and large orange berries in autumn. Although this fast growing and attractive tree provides dense shade for the agricultural crops, it is one of Madeira's invasive plants, threatening areas of natural vegetation.

Indigenous flora soon takes over as our route begins a short climb to a fine viewpoint high above the sea cliffs (Wp.2 10M); it's possible to see along the coast to **Porto Moniz**, while lying directly below is **São Cristovão** and **Boa Ventura**, our destination.

Ilhéu Preto and Ilhéu Vermelho

From this panoramic vantage point we take in the expanse of the ocean, gloriously turquoise and crystal clear with white surf breaking on the tiny islets of **Ilhéu Preto** and **Ilhéu Vermelho** just out from the coast.

At this point the path starts its steep descent, zigzagging down the almost vertical cliff; in parts, carved into the rock face; however, it is quite wide and good underfoot with railings for protection where needed.

On the approach to sea level our trail meets another path (Wp.3 30M) in front of an old stone barn. Going right here leads to the headland and the ruins of an old sugar cane mill (Wp.4 35M).

Madeira Sea Stock

Much of the vegetation along the route is typical of other coastal areas, but there are a number of exceptions; during spring and summer many endemic species are found in flower including White Everlasting, Stonecrops, Golden Musschia, Madeira Germander, Madeira Sea Stock, Carline Thistles and chrysanthemums. No one will fail to spot the magnificent specimens of Houseleek which thrive here; the disc Houseleek or

Disc Houseleek

Saucer plant (Aeonium glandulosum) clings to the rock face while the Viscid Houseleek (Aeonium glutinosum) appears everywhere along the route.

After taking that short detour and returning to the junction, our **Caminho da Entrosa** path continues in front of the old barn descending down to a stone bridge (Wp.5 43M), which we cross before climbing up to **São Cristovão**. Just before the bridge, there is another path to the right which makes a short detour beside red clay walls to more ruins at the mouth of the river, an option for anyone wanting to leave the main trail to extend the walk.

Our route continues from the bridge and climbs around 65 metres to **São Cristovão**, soon passing through denser vegetation. Towards the top, a path alongside a narrow *levada* (Wp.6 57M) leads us to **Bar Restaurante São Cristovão** (Wp.7 60M) from where we have wonderful views of the coastline and of the whole of the **Entrosa** trail as it zigzags steeply down the cliffs. To the south lie the forested slopes of the central mountain range with the full expanse of the **Ribeira Porco** valley, also in view.

.. the view west from the bar-restaurante ..

From the restaurant it's a 1.7 kilometre walk on a tarred road, climbing past agricultural buildings and new property to arrive beside an electricity tower on the regional road, close to the village centre of **Boa Ventura** (Wp.8 100M). The bus stop is directly opposite the tower.

18 PICO DO AREEIRO TO PICO RUIVO
(PR1 - VEREDA DO AREEIRO)

The most popular high altitude walk on the island links the two highest peaks of **Pico Ruivo** (1862 metres) and **Pico do Areeiro** (1817 metres). The steep, stony trail crosses the central mountain massif and is often cut across the sheer cliffs as it passes below **Pico do Gato** (1782 metres) and around **Pico das Torres** (1852 metres). It's an extremely demanding and rewarding walk, offering magnificent views; the steepness of the cliffs and the contrast in shape and colour of the rock is quite breathtaking.

High altitude routes are not suitable to walk in bad weather. An early start is recommended to avoid cloud cover which generally appears later in the day. We follow exposed, clearly defined and way-marked cobbled paths and mule trails subject to vast variations in temperature, therefore appropriate clothing and footwear are essential. The many precarious sections we meet on route are securely protected by steel posts and cable where necessary. The main route (around 3 hours/7 kilometres) follows the original path around the eastern side of **Pico das Torres**. An alternative shorter and easier option (approx. 2 hours) is to pass on the western side, negotiating five tunnels constructed at a later period, thus taking 1.4 kilometres off the journey and cutting cut out the steep ascent around **Torres**.

Numerous bird species can be spotted along the trail and this mountain area is the only known breeding site in the world of Zino's petrel, a species endemic to the island. High altitude heathland dominated by broom, bracken and grasses is home to a wealth of outstanding flora, many endemic species appearing in summer. In particular, the rare Madeira Violet or Mountain Pansy (Viola paradoxa) can be found. Other endemic species include Madeira Thrift, Eyebright, Saxifrage and Rock Orchids.

Access by hire car or taxi: take the ER103 from **Funchal** passing through **Monte** parish and continue on to the village of **Poiso**. At the road junction in **Poiso**, go left continuing on the ER202 for 7 kilometres to arrive at the **Pousada** (inn) car park at **Pico do Areeiro**.

Starting at the **Pousada** (Wp.1 0M), we firstly climb the short distance to the **Pico do Areeiro** trig point on the summit (Wp.2 3M), from where we soak in the impressive mountain scenery. The views are magnificent; stretches of our onward route crossing alongside the mountain are clearly visible. Returning towards the **Pousada**, we now follow a stone-paved path which crosses a narrow spine before descending steps to reach a wide grassy area. After a short ascent our path drops down again to arrive at the foot of a rocky outcrop, on top of which sits **Ninho da Manta** *miradouro* (Buzzard's Nest) (Wp.3 15M). We climb the steps beside the rock face; just before reaching the viewing platform our route continues climbing on

.. around Pedra Riga ..

the left. The path to the right is a short diversion to a viewing platform from where **Fajã da Nogueira** and **São Roque do Faial** are visible in the distance.

Back at the junction, our ascent now begins in earnest as we clamber up steps to

contour around **Pedra Riga** before our path veers to the right passing along a very narrow ridge (Wp.4 30M). The drops to each side are quite phenomenal but are well protected and from here we can look down on the outskirts of **Funchal**.

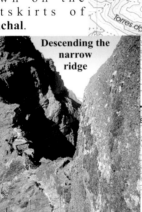
Descending the narrow ridge

Still moving along the narrow ridge, we now descend to a land mass and pass through an arch formed by a huge boulder, before arriving at a short tunnel which takes us below **Pico do Gato** (Wp.5 45M). On emerging, we have views of **Pico Grande** in the distance and, starting to descend, the **Curral** valley also comes into view. Our route descends steeply for around 158 metres before arriving at a fingerpost and junction, where the east and west paths around **Pico das Torres** separate (Wp.6 60M).

The alternative route leads off to the left, but we take the right-hand path, passing under a rock face before beginning a long and strenuous ascent around the eastern shoulder of **Pico das Torres**. This climb of 157 metres takes around 45 minutes - you'll be thankful when the path finally levels off and we arrive breathless at the top - a rest stop here is most welcome (Wp.7 105M).

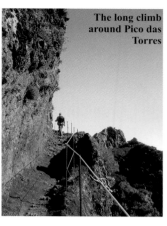

The long climb around Pico das Torres

Now following a rocky descent protected with a good handrail, we pass a stone cairn (Wp.8 115M), after which the path veers to the opposite side of the hill. Crossing over a watercourse and under another huge boulder bridge, we find amazing rock formations all around us (Wp.9 128M) before arriving at another fingerboard where the east and west trails rejoin (Wp.10 137M).

Going straight ahead, we begin to skirt the cliff edge, passing on our left a number of caves dug out of the volcanic rock. In the past these served as shelters for shepherds and as a refuge for cattle. Beyond the caves the path begins to climb gently, passing through an area of beautiful ancient heaths before the ascent steepens. For the remainder of the trail we have a long uphill slog, passing through more heaths, before finally arriving at a junction, often bustling with other walkers, just below the **Government Rest House**. There's a collection of fingerposts giving directions for all of the **Ruivo** routes, which converge at this point. Another short ascent up a zigzag stairway brings us into the courtyard of the mountain hostel (Wp.11 175M) where we can buy drinks and snacks and take a rest before the final ascent to **Ruivo** summit.

Looking across to Pico Grande

Following the directions given in Walk 20, we arrive at the trig. point (1862 metres). This magnificent *miradouro* gives us 360 degree views over the island on a clear day, and over to the **Desertas Islands** and **Porto Santo** (Wp.12 200M).

Leaving the summit we now descend to **Achada do Teixeira**, again following the directions given in Walk 20 (Wp.11 to Wp.1). This takes around 40 minutes. Alternatively, those wishing to walk back to **Pico do Areeiro**, can return by the same route, this time varying the journey by passing along the western side of **Pico das Torres** and negotiating the five tunnels along the way; allow just over two hours to return along this shorter alternative route.

Leaving Achada do Teixeira

Starting below the **Pico Ruivo** government house, this trail descends from 1700 metres, first crossing the central mountain massif before traversing through indigenous forest to end in the parish of **Ilha** above **São Jorge**, 485 metres above sea level. To reach the start we complete a two kilometer hike from **Achada do Teixeira** which includes a climb of 150 metres over approximately 1.5 kilometres; for directions to the start, follow Walk 20 (Wp.1 - Wp.5).

Though challenging, the route is well defined and signposted with the addition of red and yellow flash mark symbols, particularly on the first section. As it's very steep in parts, a walking pole is strongly recommended to ease the pressure on leg muscles and joints. Please note that, as with all high altitude routes, rapid changes in weather conditions often occur, therefore appropriate clothing and footwear should be worn.

The trail passes through herbaceous and bush vegetation, then heads into the *laurisilva* forest after descending to around 1100 metres above sea level. At **Vale da Lapa**, approximately half way, there's the option of picking up the trail of **Levada do Caldeirão Verde** which begins and ends at **Queimadas Forest Park**; refer to Walk 22.

| 5 | 4H | 10.5 km | 150m / 1215m | ⟷ | 2 |

Access by hire car or taxi: follow directions for Walk 20.

Access by bus: there's a regular bus service (Nos. 56, 103 & 138) from **Funchal** to **Santana** where taxis are then available to deliver us to our starting point at **Teixeira** car park.

The walk begins a short distance below the **Pico Ruivo** government rest house (Wp.1 30M) and follows a paved pathway leading off right from the main **Ruiva** trail. Descending over an area of rocky ground sparsely covered with bracken and heather, we soon reach a rocky outcrop (Wp.2 38M) providing

The start of the Ilha trail

wonderful mountain views. The descent then becomes steep and crosses a number of rocky water courses before negotiating a land bridge between two rises (Wp.3 50M).

Zigzagging down stone and log steps, our path crosses a 30 metre boulder field after which the stony descent gives way to denser vegetation through heaths and broom. Still descending and passing down a long section of steep and slippery log steps, we reach a finger post signed 'Pico Ruivo' and 'Semagrel' (Wp.4 73M.) Continuing ahead, we drop down another section of steps before swinging right, passing a number of small caves on the right (Wp.5 100M). As the altitude decreases, Azorean Laurels, pines and Wax Myrtle now share space with the heaths; a little later we are in the indigenous forest where Fetid Laurels, Lily of the Valley and other deciduous species also appear.

As the path bends left, we arrive at a junction with a fingerpost directing us straight ahead to the **Vale da Lapa Forestry Post**, our onward route to **Ilha**. (Wp.6 120M).

Alternative routes
At this point we have the option of taking the path to the right, descending a short distance before joining **Levada da Caldeirão Verde** close to where the channel goes into a tunnel. We then continue along the *levada* to end our walk at **Parque das Queimadas**, passing through an area of wonderful natural forest for the rest of our journey and, of course, saving any further tension on the legs. For directions back to **Queimadas** follow Walk 22. From the **Queimadas Forestry House** it is around 5 kilometres back to **Santana**.

From the junction with the *levada* it's also possible to rejoin the main **Ilha** trail a little distance below the **Vale da Lapa Forestry Post** - slightly quicker, though you'll miss out on the lovely area around the house.

Our main route however, continues from the 'Vale da Lapa' fingerpost (Wp.6) making a short ascent up to the forestry house (Wp.7 140M), an ideal place for rest and refreshments under the huge pines trees. The views from the house are stunning; **Pico Ruivo** and **Pico das Torres** soar above us while the rural areas above **Santana** and **São Jorge** are visible below.

Santana mountain range as seen from São Jorge

Descending from the forestry post, we soon encounter a series of worn stone steps and pass through an area of mixed woodland before reaching a wide track (Wp.8 174M), which we follow until it bends right, our path leading off over a grassy area (Wp.9 180M). Our route now leads us down steps into a narrow gully to reach a track at the lower level where we find another fingerpost signed 'Ermida', a village to the east of **Ilha** (Wp.10 200M). Going straight across the track, we continue over another grassy area before descending into a second deeper and longer cutting, to arrive at another track where we turn right.

A short distance along, a signpost for 'Ilha' (Wp.11 214M) directs us off left; a few minutes later we meet another sign for 'Garnel', a tiny hamlet below **Ilha**. Ignoring this we go slightly to the right, signed 'Lombado do Meio', now passing beside a narrow *levada* before dropping down a flight of steps to the end of the trail where it meets a tarred road (Wp.12 230M).

Heading down the road, it's only a short distance to the church and village centre where there's a small shop and a bar, from where we can call a taxi to take us back **Santana** or to our starting point (Wp.13 240M).

High peaks are always exhilarating, and **Pico Ruivo** has it all; spectacular views, easy access along a comfortable paved path, no precipitous drops and refreshments below the summit - the only Madeiran peak to combine all these features, making this route a must for everyone who can handle the exertion and altitude.

Access by hire car or taxi: from **Santana** centre take the ER218, which climbs up past **Pico das Pedras** reserve and forestry post and continues on through the forest, finally ending at **Achada do Teixeira** car park.

Access by bus: there is a regular bus service (Nos 56, 103 & 138) from **Funchal** to **Santana** where taxis are then available to deliver us to our starting point.

Homen em Pé,

The walk begins at the information panel (Wp.1 0M) and follows a paved pathway up the hillside, but before setting off on the ascent, we take a short detour to the **Homen em Pé**, 'The Standing Man' (Wp.2 5M).This impressive basalt formation stands on the cliff edge, beyond which are fantastic views of the north coast and **Eagle Rock**. This is accessed along a narrow path which passes in front of the **Teixeira** government house, before continuing a short distance between the heaths to arrive at the *miradouro*.

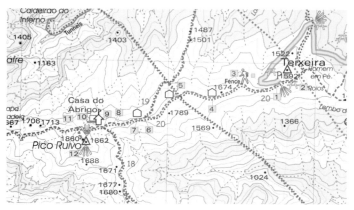

Back at the car park, our trail to **Ruivo** follows the manicured, stone-laid path which steadily climbs to a broad-backed ridge giving us superb views over the north and south valleys. A steeper section follows taking us through a gate (Wp.3 18M) before passing a cairn on our left and zigzagging to the top of the first ascent to arrive at the first stone shelter (Wp.4 26M).

The landscape is characterized by herbaceous and bush vegetation, but as we pass along the **Santana** mountain range we can see the **Queimadas** forest below, as well as the area of the interior where the **Ribeira Grande** valley emanates from **Caldeirão Verde** and **Caldeirão do Inferno**. The hamlet of **Achada do Marques** in the centre of the **Ribeira dos Acros** valley is also clearly visible along this section.

Another gentle ascent follows, bringing us to the second stone shelter (Wp.5 33M). As we cross a crest, the spectacularly sited guesthouse comes into view. Surprisingly, we now have a steady downhill stretch before arriving at a junction with our Walk 19 (PR1.1 - Vereda do Ilha) where the narrow, signed pathway descends steeply to the right (Wp.6 43M).

From here it's a steady ascent, to pass another stone shelter (Wp.7 45M) before we're looking down on the footpath coming over from **Areeiro** which edges its way around a sheer bowl surrounded by magnificent peaks; the mast close to **Areeiro** summit can also be seen from this point. Still steeply climbing, we soon pass though stone gate posts (Wp.8 52M) before the final ascent, which takes us through tall tree heaths to arrive at the junction with Walk 18, (PR1 - Vereda do Areeiro) (Wp.9 57M).

From the fingerposts a short, stepped climb brings us to the government house courtyard (Wp.10 60M), just the place to take a break before the final ascent.

The government shelter

In this splendidly isolated location, it's a wonder that the rest house offers refreshments for sale at all, considering the logistics of getting supplies here.

Built in 1939, it was later extended to include overnight accommodation for hikers, which can be arranged through the offices of the Regional Secretary for the Environment and Natural Resources 'Secretaria Regional do Ambiente e Recursos Naturais', in Edificio Golden Gate, **Funchal**.

The final ascent to the summit (1862 metres above sea level) follows a cobbled, stepped path, which starts from the courtyard and heads towards

Pico Ruivo. It is a steady, energetic climb to arrive at a junction and fingerpost below the peak (Wp.11 66M), which is the start of our Walk 21 (PR1.3 Vereda da Encumeada). Going left from the fingerpost, we now zigzag up the steep slopes, avoiding the scree shortcuts, to arrive breathless on top of **Pico Ruivo** (Wp.12 80M).

.. looking west from Pico do Ruivo ..

From the summit we enjoy spectacular 360 degree views, across the central massif as well as to part of the eastern peninsula and the **Desertas Islands;** to the north, we can also pick out the outline of **Porto Santo**, so it's no surprise that we are likely to be sharing this viewing point with plenty of other walkers.

The platforms around the trig point and across to the two extremities have recently been laid with wooden decking to avoid erosion, and the whole area has also been protected with strong fencing.

The descent back to **Teixeira** is the reverse of our climb, which is easier physically and accompanied by wonderful views along the whole of the descent to the car park (Wp.1 135M).

The last of our four trails passing through the **Pico Ruivo** area heads west across the central mountain massif to its end in **Encumeada**. Another exhilarating walk, extremely demanding and only for experienced walkers. The route is marked throughout with red and yellow flash waymarkings; difficult sections, particularly on the ups and downs, are well protected. However, as with all high mountain walks, it is very exposed and susceptible to extreme weather conditions and therefore appropriate clothing and footwear are essential as is the need to carry plenty of water. The descent towards the end is extremely steep and uneven; as a result it is not advisable to walk this route in reverse.

The trail follows a mountain path on a wide undulating ridge and is marked by a number of steep climbs and descents with elevations between 1760 and 1000 metres. Periodically the path crosses the ridge taking in panoramic views of the majestic valley of **Curral das Freiras** and the south coast as well as villages and towns of the north coastal area. Even the **Desertas Islands** and **Porto Santo** can be seen from some vantage points, cloud permitting. The final descent passes into the laurisilva forest before ending on the ER228 at the **Encumeada** pass.

The walk officially starts a short distance from the **Ruivo** Government Shelter, necessitating once again the two kilometre hike from **Achada do Teixeira**, well worth the effort to access this wonderful isolated location. For directions to the start follow Walk 20 (Wp.1 – 9 50M).

Access by hire car or taxi: from **Santana** centre take the ER218, which climbs up past the **Pico das Pedras** Forestry Post and continues through pine and eucalyptus forest, finally ending at a dirt car park at **Achada do Teixeira**.

.. our starting point ..

Access by bus: regular buses (Nºs 56, 103 & 138) run from **Funchal** to **Santana** where taxis are then available to deliver us to our start at **Teixeira** car park. There's limited service via **Encumeada** (Nº6 & 139 serving **Serra da Água** and **Santa**, **Porto Moniz**. However a more frequent service is from **Ribeira Brava** to **São Vicente** on the VE4, via the **Encumeada** tunnel.

Leaving the government shelter and passing a path on the left leading to

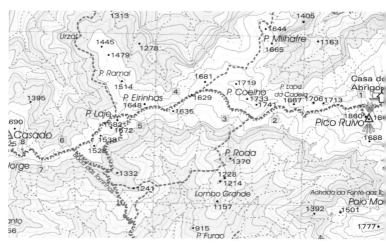

the summit of **Ruivo**, we begin our walk a few metres along (Wp.1 0M) following a good footpath, which descends down the north west flank of **Ruivo** (Wp.2 20M). Here we have our first view over to **Pico Grande**. The vegetation, although quite sparse, is interspersed with heaths and other shrubs

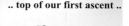
.. top of our first ascent ..

and throughout summer, carpets of mountain thyme and marjoram provide wonderful colour and scent the air. At the end of the descent the pathway changes to rougher terrain, but is well protected with metal railing where needed.

Ancient heaths

.. the spectacular Curral Valley ..

An ascent now follows, on a mixture of paved and gravel paths and soon passes through an area of ancient heaths and broom. After another hundred metres descent, the path levels off to follow the flank of a hill below **Pico Coelho** and here a disused path descends south

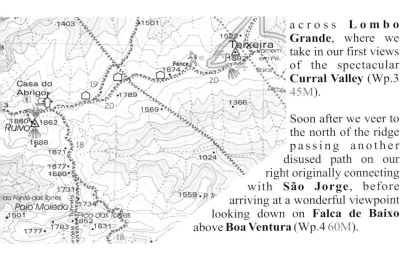

across **Lombo Grande**, where we take in our first views of the spectacular **Curral Valley** (Wp.3 45M).

Soon after we veer to the north of the ridge passing another disused path on our right originally connecting with **São Jorge**, before arriving at a wonderful viewpoint looking down on **Falca de Baixo** above **Boa Ventura** (Wp.4 60M).

Another climb and we arrive at a precipitous rocky outcrop, again affording views of 'Nun's Valley', although caution is needed here, as the outcrop is not fenced (Wp.5 75M). Just a little further along, an old path leading south into the valley forks off left while we follow the path to the right. Another four minutes along on the left, we reach a clearing in the trees obviously used for camping; note there are no facilities here.

From here we go to the right down a series of steep steps, which although well protected, are damp and slippery, so care is needed. Passing under an impressive rock face, we climb thirty metres on a very steep section up the side of the rocks before arriving at a spectacular viewpoint, where the whole depression of **Curral das Freiras** lies before us and from where, the old path is visible below. Along this section of our route, rock orchids, endemic chrysanthemums and pride of Madeira are a few of the wonderful mountain species, which can be found.

Another three minutes and we reach the junction at **Boca das Torrinhas** (Wp.6 61M) where the main pathway into the **Curral** valley leads off to the left with our route going straight ahead. Another kilometer along we pass through a cleft in the rock (Wp7 135M) before another severe climb (Wp.8 156M), where we find an interesting cave dug into the rock face. These appear periodically along the trail and were a means of refuge for men who, through necessity, had to walk this ancient trail to collect the heath for stakes, firewood and for making charcoal. Quite a contrast we imagine, to the now universal pastime of walking for pleasure.

Ascending again to the right, we soon pass a large rock and cairn to the left before arriving at a flat rocky area where we follow right, keeping the cairns to our left. Ten minutes later we meet a junction with a disused path on our left which doesn't appear on any maps though a crude sign painted on the rock suggests it once led to **Pico Grande** (Wp.9 200M).

We now pass into the natural forest and begin a long and steep descent on

uncomfortable and uneven steps making it difficult to get into any walking rhythm.

.. huge sections of black basalt cliffs ..

The total descent is around 550 metres; along the way we pass more caves, go through a number of gates and head around huge sections of black basalt cliffs before eventually joining a steep dirt track leading us past the signboard at the end of the walk, to arrive at the ER228 regional road (Wp.10 300M).

Snack Bar Encumeada can be found a few metres south of the road junction.

The municipality of **Santana** on the north coast incorporates the parishes of **Arco de São Jorge**, **São Jorge**, **Ilha**, **Faial** and **São Roque do Faial**. This agricultural area, rich in tradition, is home to the Madeira Theme Park, though the area is perhaps most well-known for its A-framed thatched cottages.

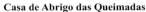

Casa de Abrigo das Queimadas

Parque das Queimadas is a lovely area situated above the agricultural lands of **Santana**. The Forestry Post, **Casa de Abrigo das Queimadas**, with original features of the typical **Santana** houses, has a marvellous thatched roof and sits proudly in the centre of the park.

A second thatched building stands close by; and even the ducks have been provided with their own traditional little houses - quite charming. The paved courtyard and picnic tables are surrounded by elegant parkland with excellent specimens of Japanese Cedars and European Beech.

Levada do Caldeirão Verde, built in the 18th century, begins in the stream bed of the **Caldeirão Verde** river and passes through cliffs and mountains as it carries water from the highest peaks to culminate in the farm lands of **Faial**; the channel also enables access into the interior of the island, providing spectacular mountainous views along the way.

Access by hire car or taxi: from the tunnel and roundabout on the VE1, follow the main access road into **Santana**. A few hundred metres along take a left turn for **Queimadas** (Opposite Hiper SA Supermarket). The road climbs for around 5 km to reach **Parque das Queimadas**.

Parque das Queimadas

Access by bus: there's a regular bus (N°s 56, 103 & 138) from **Funchal** to **Santana** from where taxis are available to deliver us to our starting point at **Queimadas** car park.

Leaving the cobbled courtyard (Wp.1 0M) and passing over a wooden bridge, we follow a well-signed route through the parkland, soon passing a track on the left where we pick up the *levada* (Wp.2 5M).

Initially the pathway is wide and laced with roots, but as we leave the formal parkland behind, the indigenous forest takes over and the channel and shoulder, carved against the rock walls, now becomes narrower. Looking to the right across the forest canopy, the small settlement of **Achada do Marques**, designated a protected site due to its traditional farm terraces and old stone cow huts, comes in to view. This pretty hamlet is located in the parish of **Ilha** and is well worth a visit.

Soon the path makes a short detour to avoid a dangerous section of the channel (Wp.3 19M), where we descend and ford a stream before ascending on the opposite side. Sections of the *levada* shoulder become quite narrow once again so we must pass in single file. However, all precipitous drops throughout the whole trail are well protected with steel posts and cable. We cross a bridge over an impressive gorge (Wp.4 30M), looking down on a green expanse of chain fern.

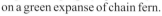
.. a magnificent waterfall ..

Rounding another bend, we find a magnificent waterfall dropping over 50 metres into a pool below the *levada* (Wp.5 55M). Big-Leaved Crowfoots and geraniums abound, the damp conditions supporting numerous ferns and moisture-loving species. We soon pass a second waterfall at another valley head (Wp.6 65M).

Moving alongside cliffs under numerous drips and sprays, we arrive at the first tunnel (Wp.7 82M); quite short but dark, a torch is useful though not essential.

Five minutes later we meet the second tunnel entrance and a junction of paths (Wp.8 87M). Our route turns left into the tunnel, while the path to the right intersects with the **Ruivo to Ilha** trail (Walk 19). This second tunnel is around 200 metres long but the path is wide, paved and has good headroom.

No sooner have we emerged than we meet the third tunnel entrance. This appears much darker due to a curve in the middle and becomes extremely low towards the end, but there are two fascinating windows cut through the rock, where we can look down into the forest.

A 'window' in the third tunnel

Emerging, (92M) we find ourselves above an enormous forest bowl. The channel shoulder narrows again as we pass through the final tunnel (Wp.9 104M), only a few metres long but it

curves in the middle and is uneven, so a torch is useful.

Our route becomes quite awesome as the path narrows yet again, with the channel cut against high rock walls and the valley to our right, unbelievably deep.

Fifteen minutes after passing through the fourth tunnel we arrive at the **Caldeirão Verde** riverbed, where we leave the *levada* and climb a few metres to reach the green pool (Wp.10 120M). We find ourselves in a magnificent basin with towering walls and exotic flora, the **Caldeirão Verde** stream falling 100 metres into the lovely green lake.

Caldeirão Verde

After indulging ourselves in these beautiful surroundings, we return to **Queimadas** (Wp.1 240M) by the same route.

Extensions

One hour's walk from the Green Pool is **Caldeirão do Inferno** where waterfalls pour into a deep dark gorge. This trail continues along the **Levada do Caldeirão Verde** before picking up **Levada do Pico do Ruivo**, then passes through several tunnels. However, it's recommended for experienced walkers only, due to the often difficult and slippery terrain and some unprotected sections along the route. Add two hours return.

For an easier extension (suitable for all abilities and an official PR JOEL route suitable for disabled people using Joelette adapted wheelchairs) we suggest starting at **Pico das Pedras** on the ER218 above **Santana**. (Access details in Walk 21). Again lying at 900 metres above sea level, the area of **Pico das Pedras** is part of the Parque Natural da Madeira and is classified as an Amenity Reserve. Begin the walk from the car park at **Rancho Madeirense** with its small thatched **Santana** houses for rent, following a broad, well-manicured woodland trail, eventually picking up the *levada*. After a total of 2 km, arrive at the cobbled road at **Queimadas**. Allow around 30 minutes additional walking time each way.

23 RIBEIRO BONITO
(PR18 - LEVADA DO REI)

The 'beautiful river' of **Ribeiro Bonito** is our destination for this lovely walk into the interior. The trail follows **Levada do Rei** along mountain slopes into a spectacular area of native forest. En-route we cross pretty streams, negotiate a short tunnel and pass behind a beautiful waterfall.

Our trail begins at the Water Treatment Plant at **Quebrados** in **São Jorge** and ends at the source of the *levada* at the head of the **Bonito** valley. Although the channel shoulder is quite narrow in places, it is well protected on all precipitous sections.

Access by hire car or taxi: take the VE1 to **Santana** and continue west on the ER101 towards **São Jorge**. On approaching the village, take a left turn at the side of a petrol station, signed 'Moinho a Água' and continue up the hill for 2.4 kilometres, taking two left turns. After passing a water mill on the right, continue for 1 kilometre to a T-Junction with a tarred forest road. Turn left here; the *levada* crosses over the road a few metres ahead.

Access by bus: there's a regular bus service (N°s 56, 103 & 138) from **Funchal** to **Santana** and **São Jorge** village where taxis are then available to take us to our starting point.

From the information board at **Quebrados** (Wp.1 0M), we follow the *levada* upstream for approximately 50 metres before bearing right into the Water Treatment Station (Wp.2 2M), passing in front of the reservoir to a fingerboard on the left. The channel gushes down a water stairway which we climb on stone and earthen steps, before our route turns left into the forest, taking us at first through pines and eucalyptus where Black Wattle Mimosa and Mauritius Nightshade are also present.

Levada do Rei

Walking through this thinner area of woodland, we soon have views across the **São Jorge** and **Santana** farmlands with the village of **Ilha** standing out on a peak in the distance and the magnificent mountain range around **Pico Ruivo** ahead. Contouring around to the **Bonito** valley, we soon encounter a path coming down from the right to cross the *levada* and descend into the valley (Wp.3 27M). Ignoring this, we continue along the channel shoulder, our trail now leading us into the spectacular native forest which becomes green, dense and humid as we progress. From here the channel constantly passes beside the rock face, water dripping into the *levada* and forested slopes rising and falling to our right and left. Shortly after we see a large waterfall in the valley to our left (Wp.4 52M); this is **Ribeira de Sebastião**, a tributary of the **Ribeiro Bonito;** a short distance ahead we cross over the river on stepping stones.

After 2.7 kilometres the *levada* meets with a broad forest maintenance track coming down right from the **Cascalha** Forestry Post. From here the track continues alongside the *levada* (Wp.5 60M). At the junction, a finger post directs our way, indicating 2.4 kilometres to the source of **Levada do Rei**. This stretch of track is wide and rather muddy in places, becoming drier again after passing a cave on our right (Wp.6 70M) before eventually petering out; we then continue again along the narrow channel shoulder. Now deep in the forest, we cross a second stream (Wp.7 80M) as we arch round into a deep valley.

Emerging from the tunnel

Walking beside a rock wall, the shoulder becomes very narrow, but is well protected. Our trail then arrives at a tunnel entrance (85M), the channel paved as it passes through it; although curved in the middle, it's only around 10 metres long so does not require a torch. Rounding yet another side valley, we pass a cairn on our left before a narrow path leading into the valley bottom drops down to the left (Wp.8 88M) accessing the eastern slopes of the **Bonito** valley where we believe it is possible to meet up with the **Ilha**, **Caldeirão Verde** and **Inferno** walking trails.

.. the beautiful Ribeiro Bonito ..

Ignoring this left hand path, we continue to follow the *levada*, within minutes reaching a beautiful waterfall at the head of this side valley (Wp.9 98M). Though at first glance quite foreboding, it's quite easy to walk behind without getting too much of a shower. The channel is paved over at this point and more protective fencing appears, making it quite safe to negotiate. Leaving the waterfall, our trail re-enters the main valley and after a further six minutes, we arrive at the beautiful **Ribeiro Bonito** stream and the source of **Levada do Rei** (Wp.10 105M).

The beauty and isolation of this location cannot be underestimated and a quote from the official PR 18 leaflet, "the sensation of having gone back in time to the discovery of the island" is an apt description.

Moinho a Água

From here we retrace our steps back to the starting point (Wp.1 210M). However, before heading off back to our base, we should allow some time to visit the **São Jorge Water Mill (Moinho a Água)**, a kilometer from the information board. This 300-year old mill is beautifully restored with original

working presses and grinders. The mill produced corn meal, wheat, barley and rye; the museum's curator, a friendly local lady, will show you around and demonstrate the processes. Fed by the **Levada do Rei**, the water can be observed through an arched opening below the building, coursing down from above and into the basement.

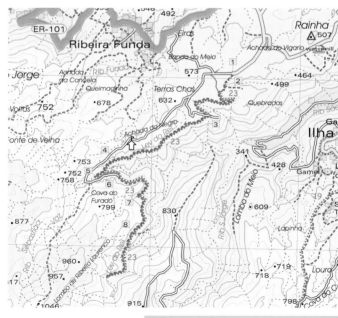

One of three trails starting in **Ribeiro Frio**, we follow a beautiful scenic route to one of Madeira's most spectacular *miradouro* viewpoints. A short walk with good pathways and no precipitous drops, it's recommended for all. The best time to visit is during spring and summer when the flora is at its best and there's less chance of cloud invading the valley, blocking out the views.

Ribeiro Frio is one of the most popular tourist destinations on the island due to its stunning location below high peaks whilst nestling within the largest area of natural forest on the island. The centre boasts attractions including gift shops and restaurants as well as a trout farm and nature reserve, where many rare endemic forest plants are cultivated for display.

Access by hire car or taxi: take the ER103 to **Ribeiro Frio**. Car drivers can park near the bars, or lower down the road near the **Balcões** path, or at the picnic areas at the top end of the village. Although buses N°s 103 and 138 go to **Ribeiro Frio**, they are few and not conveniently timed for walking excursions, so are not recommended.

From the settlement's two bars we walk down the road until it swings left; here an information board on the corner marks the start of our broad path (Wp.1 0M). Following **Levada Velha**, we head into the shady forest before meandering round the first valley head where we cross over a bridge (Wp.2 6M).

Along this stretch the path winds away from the ER103 which can be seen descending the valley; looking eastwards, there's a rare opportunity to appreciate the scale and density of the *laurisilva*, its canopy rising over the eastern mountain slopes. This is a wonderful location for escaping the heat of the summer and the vegetation is superb. Endemic species abound, including Rock Orchids (Orchis scopulorum) Madeira Stonecrop (Aichryson divaricatum) and Black Parsley (Melanoselinum decipiens) with its large trunk and umbel flower heads.

After ten minutes the route passes through a high rock cutting (Wp.3 12M) then alongside rugged slopes, giving views down to **Faial**, before reaching the small log cabin of **Bar Flor da Selva** (Wp.4 18M) where you can stop for a drink or buy souvenirs, home made wines and plants. The channel passes through another rock cutting (Wp.5) before swinging left to arrive at a junction (Wp.6 23M) where 'Balcões' is signed along the right hand cobbled path. In two minutes we arrive at a spectacularly sited viewpoint standing on a rocky outcrop, paved and protected by rustic fencing (Wp.7 25M). Mists permitting, we can look down into the **Metada Valley**, with **Penha d'Águia** to the north and the central

The junction at Wp.6

.. at a spectacular viewpoint ..

mountain range to the west. In the valley bottom is the generating station of **Fajã de Nogueira**, providing water and electricity for **Santana**, with **Levada Pico Ruivo** and **Levada da Serra** forming straight lines along the forest slopes. After

A mountain view from the viewpoint

soaking up these magnificent views, we return by the same route. However, there's the option of continuing a little further from the junction (Wp.7), following the broad tree-shaded path, until a narrow track drops into the steep valley on our right (Wp.8).

From here the path narrows and goes onto a paved and vertiginous section of the water channel, which is precipitous and dangerous. Do <u>not</u> go beyond this point.

Extension:
Once back in **Ribeiro Frio** we can take the path leading behind **Victor's Bar** where we can find many more endemic plants including the rare Yellow Foxglove (Isoplexis sceptrum) Madeira Betony (Teucrium abutiloides) and Madeira Elder.

Other endemic specimens can be seen at the **Posto Florestal Nature Reserve** adjacent to the **Fish Hatchery** (where rainbow trout are produced to replenish Madeira's watercourses) on the right of the road above the bars. A number of rare species that are quite difficult to spot in their natural habitat within the forest are grown in the reserve; we can find wild orchids (picture, page 12) Carrot Trees, Muschia wollastonii and Madeira Ironwort, making this extension a must for those interested in

Levada do Furado is one of Madeira's most well-trodden walking routes, first passing through an exceptional area of natural forest, then entering the enchanting areas of **Lamaceiros** waterhouse and forestry post before making its descent to the **Portela** viewpoint.

The first part of the trail is humid and there is little light, yet during spring and early summer, wild flowers flourish beneath the tree canopy, bringing colour and contrast in the sub-tropical forest. Later the trail crosses sunny slopes with panoramic views of the mountains and the northern coastline.

This moderately strenuous walk negotiates a series of short tunnels en route (be sure to carry a torch). Whilst there are some precipitous places, possibly a problem for vertigo sufferers, these are protected with fencing and vegetation, making it completely safe for walkers. (Note: at the time of printing the *levada* was closed for maintenance, therefore improvements in pathways and fencing are likely to have been made).

The sign at
the start (Wp.1)

Access by car: for directions to the starting point follow Walk 24 - Vereda dos Balcões (PR11).

Starting just below **Victor's Bar** (Wp.1 0M), a sign directs us over the **Ribeiro Frio** (Cold River) onto a cool, tree-shaded path, at first smooth underfoot, later becoming lumpy with tree roots and rocks.

After passing through a rock cutting (Wp.2 15M) we reach the first of several sections where the *levada* is protected by steel supports and wires (Wp.3), soon arriving at **Cabeço Pessequeiro**, where we enjoy our first views over the north coast (Wp.4).

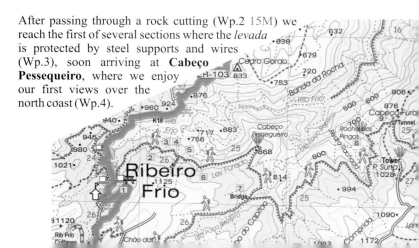

The rock cutting, Wp.2

Passing beside a tunnel bored into the hillside and a stream feeding the *levada* (Wp.5 20M), we progress a little further along to another opening in the canopy providing more views north (Wp.6 25M), just before a waterfall. As the water channel starts to curve right, the sound of rushing water meets us as we stroll along to a noisy *levada* junction by a bridge over the **Ribeiro do Bezerro** (Wp.7 52M). So many walkers take a break at this bridge that the birds expect a snack and will swoop down to beg crumbs, almost perching on your hand.

At this point our Walk 26 Ribeiro Frio Circular Tour heads off right to ascend into the forest, but for this trail we cross over the bridge to follow the broad path along the slopes, soon making the first of a number of detours below damaged sections of the *levada*. Dropping down the first stony slope, we cross a stream bed and later descend again to a lovely little pool. In late summer, if you're lucky, you could spot the very rare Yellow Foxglove (Isoplexis secptrum) growing here in the ravines and up the rocky slopes.

The walk takes on a different perspective as we wind our way through a rocky gorge where the path drops down a rock staircase to pass below cliffs, before ascending another stair back up to the channel. Soon reaching a promontory off the *levada* (Wp.8 112M), we can walk out for a few metres to enjoy views from **Rocha dos Pingos** down over the north coast.

Back on the water channel, we then arrive at a short tunnel (Wp.9 118M) where old paths go left at each end and double back over the channel; this is an alternative route up to the **Pico do Suna** water tower and viewpoint (See Walk 27).

The section of tunnels and archways now follows as we curve around the **Cabeço Furado** escarpment before we eventually arrive at the

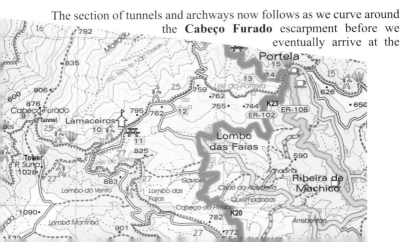

Lamaceiros waterhouse

Lamaceiros waterhouse. This tall structure, built in 1906, stands in an enchanting area surrounded by large oak trees.

Another couple of minutes along brings us to a walking crossroads (Wp.10 155M) signed 'Pico do Suna' right,

Lamaceiros forestry house gardens

'Santo da Serra' straight ahead (5km), 'Ribeiro Frio 8km' and 'Portela' left. Our route to **Portela** drops down on an earthen forest track before veering off left again on a semi-stepped path alongside the **Levada do Portela**. At the bottom of the descent, we enter the attractive gardens of the **Lamaceiros** forestry house (Wp.11 160M), with its magnificent cedars, tropical tree ferns and log-furnished picnic tables.

Leaving the gardens, we follow the forest road downhill until we reach a

.. spectacular views of Porto da Cruz ..

junction (Wp.12 172M), where our route is signed off left (PR10 Portela - 1.7km).

Now in open sunshine, we pass beside the large, fenced agricultural development of **Lombo dos Faias** with pastureland, slopes and spectacular views of **Porto da Cruz**, to our left.

At a derelict water house on our right (Wp.13 194M) the *levada* divides; a narrow channel shoots left downhill and we follow this on a log-stepped descent.

Soon entering an area of mature pines and a hedge of Madeira Juniper, we drop down a flight of earthen steps to arrive on the ER102 road beside an information panel (Wp.14 204M). Turning left here, our trail ends at the **Portela** viewpoint, bar/restaurant and taxi stand (Wp.15 210M). 150 metres downhill will bring us to the bus stop opposite the **Portela A Vista** bar.

Ribeiro Frio is one of the most popular tourist destinations on the island, due to its beautiful setting and the environmental heritage of the village; so whatever time of year you visit, it will undoubtedly be thronging with cars, coaches, buses and tourists, as will be the *levada* trails leading to **Portela** and **Balcões**. Offering an alternative for those wishing to get away from the 'madding crowds' and enjoy the peace and solitude of this stunning location and with access from the *levada* and from the road, both hidden, you are only likely to meet walkers 'in the know' along this route.

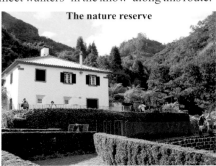

The nature reserve

Taking in a section of **Levada do Furado**, a little-known woodland climb alongside a rushing water channel, a beautiful river setting, an ascent onto the plains and a descent on a cobbled donkey trail, we then end at the nature reserve and village centre.

The initial ascent through the forest of around 330 metres is quite strenuous and definitely not recommended if wet; make this a good weather route only.

Access by car: park near **Victor's Bar**, lower down the road near the **Balcões** path (Walk 24), or at the picnic areas at the top end of **Ribeiro Frio**.

Access by bus: although buses 103 and 138 go to **Ribeiro Frio**, they are few and not conveniently timed for walking excursions, so are not recommended.

Taking the paved path below **Victor's Bar** signed 'PR10 Portela 11km' (Wp.1 0M), we cross over the river and continue as far as the bridge at **Ribeiro do Bezerro**. (See the description in Walk 25 'Ribeiro Frio to Portela' (Wps. 1-7 52M).

The path below Victor's Bar

The route to **Portela** (Walk 25) carries on over the bridge, but we clamber up to the rushing water channels to follow the higher channel straight uphill. We have a stiff and wet climb up through the forest on the narrow path alongside the rushing water channel. Some stone-laid sections of path remain, and log steps help with the ascent as ferns and mosses abound beside the path. The gradient eases (Wp.8 70M), allowing us to walk rather than climb for a section, before the ascent is rejoined. Leaks and collapsed walls on the rushing water channel mean that much of this path is wet, even in the driest of weather. This is certainly a 'huff & puff'ascent needing plenty of rests, as we progress past a cave (Wp.9 80M) and a spur of rock (Wp.10 90M).

The relentless ascent finally eases as we cross a small stream, and a path goes up to the right (Wp.11 100M); the water channel has branches bridged across it at this point. After a couple of minutes of easy walking, we are negotiating the end of the water channel and the polished rocks of **Ribeiro do Bezerro** (Wp.12 120M), an idyllic hideaway in which to take a break after that energetic climb. Refreshed, we set off on the second stage of our tour by retracing our steps back to the path junction (Wp.11 122M).

.. onto a sloping meadow ..

Turning uphill over the *levada*, we are back to climbing steeply in an almost ladder-like ascent through the trees to reach a crest (125M). After a short drop, we ascend again before clambering over rocky water run-offs (130M), then climb to emerge from the tree heather onto a sloping meadow (135M).

Suddenly we find ourselves out in the open; looking around, there is absolutely no sign of human habitation except for a flattened grass trail leading up the meadow past a stone cairn (Wp.13). We ascend the path, the slope more extreme than it first appears, through bracken and tree heather onto a col (Wp.14 140M). At last the climb is over, as we swing right towards farm buildings, the path confused by goat trails, before we come onto a surprising green grass road in front of the farm.

Turning right, we stroll along the grass track, worn areas revealing this to be a broad cobbled road, though why such a well-constructed route should exist in this isolated region is a mystery. As we head along, it is all too easy to miss the path junction (Wp.15 150M) where we go left on a narrower rippled cobbled path, to descend through a gate. Negotiating hairpin bends between tree heathers we soon encounter large rocks beside a spring (165M); squeezing through, our cobbled trail continues down to a few concrete steps to join the ER103 road; the older trail obliterated from this point (Wp.16 168M).

Heading down the road for a couple of minutes we now take a sharp left,

turning off onto a cobbled trail (170M). Once again we're descending through forest, passing earthen roads off to our left, before coming alongside the stepped *levada* above the forestry reserve and trout hatchery at **Ribeiro Frio** (Wp.17 180M). A couple of minutes downhill brings us to some well-earned refreshments at the bar of our choice, back at our starting point.

The trout hatchery

Levada da Serra extends 27 kilometres from its source in **Lamaceiros**, north-east of **Santo da Serra**, ending in **Choupana** above **Funchal**, and en route passes through the famous wicker town of **Camacha**. Much of this irrigation channel passes through the pine forests along the island's southern slopes, providing little opportunity for views; nevertheless this *levada* continues to be a well-trodden route, particularly by organized walking parties.

We have chosen a linear route taking in the final section between **Lamaceiros** and **Santo da Serra**, where the coniferous forest merges with the *laurisilva*; the ancient pines and cedars are quite spectacular. The trail has optional starting points, either from the **Portela** viewpoint or from **Santo da Serra**, depending on one's preference for uphill or downhill routes, and includes a short extension up to the **Pico do Suna** fire watch tower which sits on a promontory thrust out of Madeira's northern escarpment.

Access by car: park at **Portela** and take a taxi back from **Santo da Serra**, or vice versa.

Starting out from the convivial surroundings of **Portela**, (Wp.1 0M), we walk north up the ER102 to the PR10 information panel (Wp.2 5M),

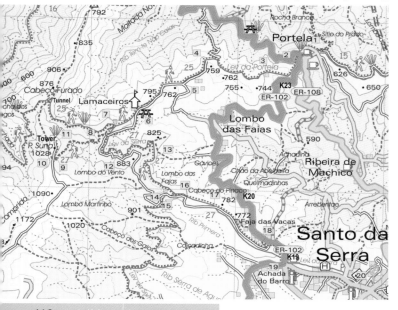

where we take the uphill path - Walk 25 'Ribeiro Frio to Portela ' in reverse. A steady but strenuous ascent brings us up through large pines to a gentler ascent, before a log-stepped climb up to the ruined building at the *levada* junction (Wp.3 20M). Turning right, we have extensive views over the north coast followed by pleasant woodland, as we follow the *levada* to contour around the hillside until we come to a dirt road (Wp.4 40M).

The road passes beside the fenced agricultural area of **Lombo das Faias**, eventually meeting a junction (Wp.5 50M) where we go uphill to a second junction, continuing climbing to the attractive

Lamaceiros forestry post

gardens and forestry post at **Lamaceiros** (Wp.6 60M).

Its log stools and tables and sub-tropical flowers make this a pleasant spot in which to recover from the climb.

Log furniture under a majestic tree

Taking a path and log stairway at the top end of the gardens, we follow **Levada da Portela** which ascends to a walking cross roads (Wp.7 75M) where 'Pico do Suna' is signed left up a grassed-over dirt road. It's a reasonably steep ascent up the tree-covered hillside, passing through the remains of a fence (Wp.8 85M), just after a stand of soaring mature pines. It's onwards and upwards, with laurel and tree heather beginning to replace the pines as we gain height.

Shortly we take a footpath which climbs steeply up on our right (Wp.9 105M) to come onto a continuation of the forest track by a spring (Wp.10 107M). (If you miss this path, you can continue up the green road to a junction and go right to find the spring.)

There's still some ascending to do, as we go right to reach the peak (Wp.11 120M), (1047 metres altitude), just before an impressive green fire watch tower on **Pico do Suna**. The tree heather in front of the tower has been cut back to form a *miradouro* viewpoint to where the massive bulk of **Penha d'Águia** (Eagle Rock) towers over **São Roque** and **Porto da Cruz**, a fitting reward for our energetic climb.

Retracing our steps, we descend to re-join **Levada da Serra**, our route turning right to follow the channel downstream (Wp.7 150M). Soon the path sweeps right after bridging a tunnel and passing beside an enormous cedar (Wp.12 160M). Continuing, we find ourselves amongst more ancient cedars, their trunks magnificent art forms. Our stroll brings us through the dappled shade of deep woodland before squeezing round a huge boulder, as our path drops down from the channel at a landslip section, then climbs back up to it (Wp.13).

Passing a filtration point, we soon reach the **Santo da Serra** water house, illuminated by beams of sunlight (Wp.14 183M). If you've enjoyed the trees so far, you'll love the specimens beside the water-house.

Santa da Serra waterhouse

Signs on the water-house show 'Lamaceiros 3km, Portela 5km, Ribeiro Frio 12km' to the west, 'João Ferino 5km, Camacha 15km' signed east, and 'Santo da Serra 2km'.

Just past the water-house we leave the channel (Wp.15 185M) to go left down a broad track, which leaves the woodland behind. Our route comes alongside a dry water channel before it swings right to join another dirt road.

Here we leave the track (Wp.16 190M) to follow the path beside the dry water channel, down through groves of soaring eucalyptus trees. The paths widen into a logging track running down to a chain serving as a vehicle barrier (Wp.17 198M). Stepping over the chain, we come onto the dirt road to continue gently downhill past logging tracks; after passing a house, the road becomes surfaced.

Now we have an easy stroll down the lane before dropping onto the ER102 regional road (Wp.18 210M) where we enjoy views over the rich valley. Heading towards the church of **Santo António da Serra**, we turn left at the ER207 junction (Wp.19 215M), where we find the **Casa Bareto** bar convenient for refreshments. It's then a further ten minutes stroll through the outskirts of this affluent town, into the central square of **Santo da Serra**, with its taxi rank and bus stop (Wp.20 225M).

Alternative walk
To extend this walk by continuing on to **Camacha** (15 km) or to the end of the *levada* at **Choupana** (22 km), keep following the channel beyond the **Santa da Serra** water house, ignoring the forest track (Wp.15), where the official route heads off to the centre of **Santo da Serra**.

The valley of **Rabaçal** on the western slopes of the **Paúl da Serra** plateau is one of the most beautiful locations on the island as well as one much frequented by walkers. The busy car park alongside the ER110 is the starting point for around eight trails in this vicinity so whenever you visit, you are likely to find it bustling with tourists and hikers. The viewpoint from the car park is stunning, taking in the deep-forested valley, with the **Rabaçal** forestry post nestling 220 metres below. This is our destination and the starting point for this walk.

Levada das 25 Fontes is probably the most well-known and well-walked trail in this area. However, it should be noted that sections of the *levada* shoulder are extremely narrow and precipitous and, whilst these sections are well protected with steel posts and fencing, the Forestry Service issues a warning that the PR6 can cause vertigo and people should not lean or put weight on the protective barriers. Nevertheless, by using common sense and remaining alert to this advice, it's a superb walk that can be enjoyed by most people.

If you seek peace and tranquility, we suggest visiting early in the morning or later in the day, to avoid the crowds. For this reason, our return route takes us on a more tranquil yet exciting journey through the **Calheta** tunnel, terminating at a picnic and barbeque site on the ER211 above **Calheta**.

Access by hire car or taxi: the viewpoint, lies at 1290 metres above sea level and is situated on the ER110 approximately 4.5 kilometres west of the **Paúl da Serra** crossroads. From the car park we have the option to walk down the tarred access road (1.8 km taking around 25 minutes) or to take the shuttle bus, which operates daily (except Christmas Day), from 9.30 a.m. until 6.30 p.m. running at approximately 20 minute intervals. Note that, if you follow the alternative tunnel return route, you will need to organise transport in advance from its end or walk the two kilometres back to the start.

Our walk begins at the end of the access road a few metres above the Forestry House, where a sign for '25 Fontes and Risco Waterfall' appears (Wp.1 0M). Going right here, we descend a paved path through shady woodland, arriving after ten minutes at another sign directing us left to 'Levada das 25 Fontes' (Wp.2 10M). This stone-laid path drops steadily as a stepped descent through the tree-covered side of the valley, before levelling out to contour around the valley wall, then descends again to reach a T-junction on the path beside the **Levada das 25 Fontes** (Wp3 25M). Now at an altitude of 950 metres, the vegetation begins a transition from Heath Forest to laurisilva.

Turning right, we follow the *levada* upstream and after five minutes cross over the deep gorge of **Ribeira Grande** (Wp.4 30M). Soon after we descend a series of steps and leave the *levada* for a short time, before ascending on the opposite side of the gorge to pick it up again at a small water station.

The Levada das 25 Fontes

Now sections of the channel shoulder become narrow, though it is well protected and dense vegetation provides some security from the vertiginous drops. In a number of places the pathway is single file, so be prepared for long crocodiles of walking parties passing in both directions which can delay progress. Along this stretch, gaps in the vegetation allow magnificent views down the **Ribeira da Janela** valley. In a further 25 minutes we round a bend, arriving at an amphitheatre where the cliff face towers above us and the 25 natural springs cascade into a small lake at the base of the cliffs (Wp.5 60M).

One of the 25 springs at the base of the cliffs

Here we can scramble over large boulders in an area of lush green ferns and other indigenous vegetation.

Retracing our steps back to the junction where we joined the *levada*, we soon pass a track on our right (Wp.6 70M), which descends deeper into the valley to join **Levada da Rocha Vermelha**, an adventurous option for

anyone with excess energy. However, we continue on to the junction (Wp.3 95M) from where the Forestry Service Trail (PR6) now returns to the starting point, while we take an alternative route, continuing to stroll westwards on the broad

woodland path beside **Levada das 25 Fontes**. Further on, we meet a stone-laid path climbing up from the right (Wp.7), the end of the trail from **Levada da Rocha Vermelha**. Just past this point, more stone and earth steps climb up left to reach the Forestry Post.

The water house near the Calheta slopes

Continuing beside the fast running water, our trail passes through a rock cutting (Wp.8), followed by more stone steps to our left (Wp.9), before arriving at the entrance to the **Calheta** Tunnel (Wp10 115M). 800 metres in length, it takes 15 minutes to negotiate. A torch is definitely needed and possibly a sweater, depending on the weather, but the interior is clean and dry except for an occasional puddle on the path and it is wide with good headroom. The area at the entrance of the tunnel provides an impressive setting and is another jewel in the walk. To the left, water gushes down a channel to feed the *levada*, there is a lovely little shrine set into the rock and, with stone seating and the lush vegetation around the platform, it's an ideal picnic place.

The tunnel exit is a wide fern-covered chamber with trickling water; just beyond is a small water house at the head of the valley (Wp11 135M), a memorable spot with wonderful views down the **Calheta** slopes.

In the distance we can see **Levada da Rocha Vermelha**, which has also been channelled through a tunnel at a lower level and also **Levada Nova** further down still. All these channels feed the **Calheta** Hydropower Station and also provide essential water for irrigation on the south coast.

From here we follow a broad track to the right for ten minutes, which brings us to the end of our walk at the picnic site on the ER211 (Wp.12 150M). Transport should be arranged for collection at this point, the alternative being to walk or hitch hike the two kilometers back to the start.

This short forest walk to an impressive waterfall is a must for anyone wanting to discover Madeira's interior without too much exertion. At **Risco**, the **Ribeira Grande** plunges 100 metres down a sheer rock face from **Lagoa do Vento**, before falling a further 100 metres down to **Levada das 25 Fontes** and then continuing into the **Ribeira da Janela** valley to the northwest. The route to this beauty spot is well-trodden and a favourite amongst visitors to the island, so whatever time of year you visit, you won't be alone.

The descent to Rabaçal Forestry Post

Access by hire car or taxi: for directions to **Rabaçal** car park and viewpoint see Walk 28.

From the vehicle barrier on the right of the car park (Wp.1 0M), we have the option of walking down the tarred road to the **Rabaçal** Forestry Post or taking the shuttle bus; our choice for this otherwise short route, is to go on foot.

Descending through the forest, the trail twists and bends as it contours the valley head, soon crossing **Ribeira do Alecrim** which flows from the **Paúl da Serra** plateau, forming a pretty roadside pool (Wp.2 10M). The vegetation on the descent is predominantly heather and bilberry interspersed with broom and the occasional laurel, together creating a reasonably low, yet extremely dense forested area. This initial descent takes around 25 minutes

The fingerpost at Wp.6

On reaching the Forestry Post (Wp.3 25M) we descend a short flight of steps to the side of the building, turning immediately right to drop down a path into the forest to reach a junction with a dirt track alongside **Levada do Risco** (Wp.4 30M). Going right again, we soon meet another track coming down from the right (Wp.5 35M); this is our return route, but for now we continue to follow the channel against the water flow, passing a finger post on our left signed 'Levada das 25 Fontes' (Wp.6 40M). Ignoring this, we carry on alongside the channel, the damp

Anemone-Leaved Cranes-Bill

conditions ideal for numerous varieties of ferns, mosses and grasses. In spring or summer we can expect to see a number of endemic species including the wonderful Shrubby Sow Thistle, Anemone-Leaved Cranes-Bill, Madeira Orchids, Canary Buttercups

.. the waterfall crashes down ..

and Madeira Moneywort. This section offers beautiful views down the **Ribeira da Janela** valley with **Levada das 25 Fontes** and **Levada da Rocha Vermelha** clearly visible in the valley below. Twenty minutes after the sign, we arrive in the semi-circular basin of **Risco** waterfall to admire this spectacular natural landmark from the viewpoint (Wp.7 60M). The waterfall crashes down the volcanic rock face, disappearing from view into the valley far below.

From this point the *levada* shoulder is no longer passable, but can be seen as it tunnels into the rock, leading behind the waterfall and then on through further tunnels around the wooded rock face.

Impressive throughout the year, the waterfall is particularly spectacular in winter, following heavy rain. The pathway along the whole route is protected with rustic fencing on the exposed sections and, approaching the waterfall viewpoint, steel posts and fencing have been added.

Returning to our starting point, we now retrace our steps to the fork where the *levada* flows off to our right and from here continue on the higher path back to the Forestry Post (Wp.3 90M). The walk to the car park and viewpoint is 1.8 kilometres, climbing 220 metres; it's not surprising that most people take the easy option of riding back from here by bus.

At the top of the **Rabaçal** access road is one of the island's newest water channels, **Levada do Alecrim**, completed in 1961 and feeding into a holding tank for the **Calheta** Hydropower Station, on the opposite side of the ER110 road. This gives us access to a spectacular gorge with an impressive waterfall and clear blue pool, perfect for picnics, feeding the trout or swimming during the warmer months.

The reservoir & Nossa Sra de Fátima Chapel

Clearly visible from the car park, the trail follows an almost straight line through the forest and maintains height along the contours of the hillside, taking in a lovely water stairway along its route.

It's an easy walk with the exception of one or two unprotected sections, though these are no deterrent to the masses of daily visitors to this location.

1   2H   6 km   20m / 20m   1   0

Access by hire car or taxi: for directions to **Rabaçal** car park and viewpoint follow Walk 28, turning into the access road and parking on the grass below the junction. (Wp.1 0M)

From the road barrier, our well-trodden path leads off right (Wp.2); we follow it for 50 metres before meeting the *levada* path, then follow this left (Wp.3 2M). The channel shoulder provides a comfortable although quite stony path, framed by tree heather which unfortunately obscures most of the views along the initial section until the *levada* sweeps north-west, when breaks in the vegetation provide wonderful views down the valley.

Ribeira da Janela Valley

Heading off against the water flow, we pass occasional slabs bridging the channel, one of which leads to a weather station (Wp.4 10M), before passing a water collection pool teeming with trout (Wp.5 13M) beside the **Ribeira do Alecrím**, its waters diverted into the pool.

Across the river, our easy path continues past a spring (Wp.6) before coming to a viewpoint (Wp.7 18M), which overlooks our start point. A little further along, our trail passes through a couple of rock cuttings (Wp.8 20M) where there are a number of precipitous sections, but the path is quite wide and the lush vegetation gives a sense of security. At the half way point we reach a spectacular water stairway (Wp.9 25M) where the *levada* rushes down a steep chute from its higher level. After climbing to the top we are rewarded with further magnificent views down the valley.

Levada do Alecrim

The *levada* above the stairway narrows noticeably from this point, as we curve towards the **Ribeira Grande** gorge, crossing another short unprotected section (Wp.10) before the easy walking continues. From here we

have views of the gentle rolling hilltops which rise above the tree line changing colour dramatically with the seasons. If you're extremely observant along this section, you may spot the junction with our Walk 31 to **Lagoa do Vento**, the path descending from the channel shoulder to the forest below (Wp.11). Continuing, we soon meet tiny channels and streams feeding the *levada* (Wp.12 43M) and five minutes later, cross a water runoff where care is needed (Wp.13 48M).

a spectacular water stairway

Looking down to our left at this point, we see a large green pool below us

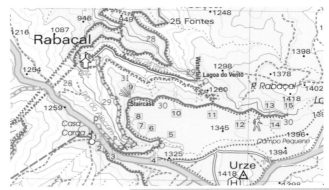

(Wp.14) and rounding a bend, we eventually arrive at the beautiful gorge, pool and river bed of **Ribeira Grande** (Wp.15 53M). Take time to relax and absorb the experience before retracing your steps.

The ribeira Grande waterfall

Ribeira Grande, also referred to as **Ribeira Lajeado**, cascades down from **Pico Rabaçal** and the area of **Lajeado**. Where the name changes, we are not sure, but from this point the river is referred to as **Ribeira Grande** until it reaches the valley floor and feeds into the **Ribeira da Janela** heading north.

This unforgettable walk is nevertheless one of Madeira's lesser known routes. Starting at **Rabaçal** on **Paúl da Serra**, we follow a level *levada* path before descending the plateau's western slopes to arrive at the small lake of **Lagoa do Vento** (Lake of the Wind), a most beautiful location deep in the forest.

Lagoa do Vento

The lake is carved into the surrounding cliffs from where the **Ribeira Grande** cascades down before falling over the rocky slopes of the **Risco** cliffs. Surrounded by natural forest, it's a wonderful place for a picnic and is ideal for swimming in summer. There's the added bonus that, due to its isolated location and less than easy access, you are likely to have it all to yourselves, unlike the pools at **Ribeira Grande** and **25 Fontes**.

The terrain leading to the lake is rocky and steep and can be very wet and slippery, particularly when crossing the many stream beds along the route, therefore it is not advisable to consider this route in wet weather. The overall descent is around 280 metres and a walking pole is definitely recommended; yet there's a great sense of achievement when completed.

Access by car: start at **Rabaçal** car park and viewpoint. Follow the directions for Walk 30.

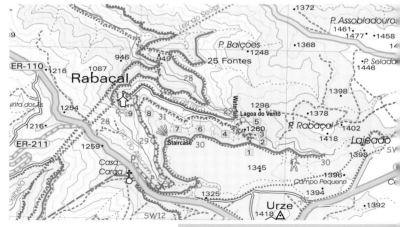

Leaving the road barrier at **Rabaçal** car park, we follow **Levada do Alecrim**, also referred to as **Levada da Ribeira Grande**. (Refer to Walk 30 Wps. 1-11). Passing the trout pond and curving around the head of the valley, we soon arrive at the water stairway and ten to fifteen minutes later, meet the path to **Lagoa do Vento** on our left (Wp.1 45M).

Descending deep into the heath forest, the trail winds and falls on a clearly defined path, passing a rocky outcrop with views down the valley before veering left and descending to a junction with a right hand path (Wp.2 52M). We ignore this and follow the main route as it descends sharply left to arrive a few minutes later at yet another junction with a right hand path (Wp.3 57M), which we again ignore.

The path now becomes extremely craggy as we scramble down, sometimes holding on to tree roots and branches for support. From here, we start to round a number of small gorges and ford the narrow streams. Soon the path zigzags with the red clay underfoot becoming quite slippery, particularly around the streams. After another fifteen minutes we hear the sound of a waterfall and close by, arrive at a third junction (Wp.4 75M). A blue hat symbol has been painted onto a rock here, and the path leading off to the right now leads us down to **Lagoa do Vento**.

Following the narrow path in the direction of the waterfalls, which immediately come into view, we look down to our left to get our first glimpse of the small green lake below us. Passing over the first waterfall's stream bed, we can now see the full extent of the magnificent valley below us. Moving on towards the **Ribeira Grande** waterfall, the path starts a winding descent down to the lake and, although quite steep, it is not too difficult.

.. proliferation of huge Sow Thistles ..

The rewards on reaching the pool make our efforts worthwhile; the lake nestles below the towering cliffs and is surrounded by lush green vegetation; the water is crystal clear (Wp.5 85M). Here we can enjoy our packed lunch and a swim if the weather is not too cold. Surprisingly we find that at some stage we had left the heath forests behind and are now in an area of *laurisilva*, with many exotic and endemic species around us. The most noticeable is the proliferation of huge Sow Thistles (Sonchus fruticosus) - quite outstanding.

Reluctantly we leave this little piece of paradise to head back to the blue hat junction (Wp.4 105M), and continue on our trail towards the **Rabaçal Forestry** house.

This area of forest consists of Tils, Azorean Laurels, Lily of the Valley trees and heathers as well as the endemic Madeira Holly (Ilex maderensis). Flowering species include the Anemone-Leaved Crane's Bill, Chrysanthemum, Big-Leaved Thistle and Bastard Hare's Ear, a dominant plant of this area.

We've now completed the steepest part of the descent, but nevertheless, the path continues over quite craggy terrain, with a particularly steep section (Wp.6 115M) where we scramble down deep steps holding on to the trees for balance, again while crossing many tiny streams. The forest at this point is dense as we pass beside a deep gorge walking almost vertically above the **Levada do Risco** path (Wp.7 135M), but another ten minutes along, the trees open up to give us magnificent views down the **Janela Valley**.

From here the gradient eases. Twenty minutes later we drop down a banking onto the **Forestry House Road** (Wp.8 155M), to the bemusement of other walkers returning from the more conventional trails. Here, we have the option of ascending the one and half kilometers of road back to the **Rabaçal** car park, or turning right to descend down to the house and the return shuttle bus (Wp.9 165M).

Alternative:
Starting from the **Rabaçal Forestry Post**, the path to **Lagoa do Vento** is picked up approximately 500 metres from the house on the left of the road, just beyond a rustic fenced view point on the right. This is a there-and-back walk, which is only slightly shorter but avoids the necessity of the main descent from **Levada do Alecrim**.

Boca da Encumeada sits at the head of a great rift, dividing the island at an almost central point. The highest peaks lie to the east with the plateau of **Paúl da Serra** to the west.

At Lombo do Mouro

From this beautiful viewpoint both south and west coastlines are visible, provided you visit in the morning; later in the day mists tend to sneak in and drape the summit with a white blanket of cloud, contrasting sharply with the lush green vegetation and black volcanic peaks.

| 4 | 5½ H | 14 km | 170m / 470m | 2 | 1 |

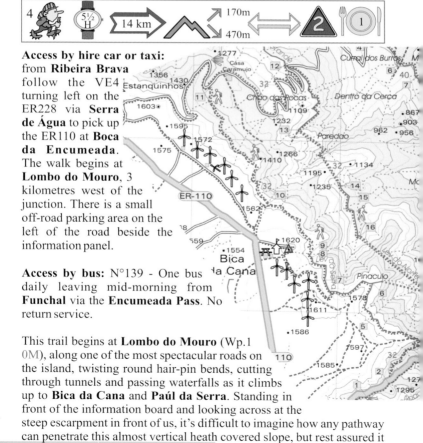

Access by hire car or taxi: from **Ribeira Brava** follow the VE4 turning left on the ER228 via **Serra de Água** to pick up the ER110 at **Boca da Encumeada**. The walk begins at **Lombo do Mouro**, 3 kilometres west of the junction. There is a small off-road parking area on the left of the road beside the information panel.

Access by bus: N°139 - One bus daily leaving mid-morning from **Funchal** via the **Encumeada Pass**. No return service.

This trail begins at **Lombo do Mouro** (Wp.1 0M), along one of the most spectacular roads on the island, twisting round hair-pin bends, cutting through tunnels and passing waterfalls as it climbs up to **Bica da Cana** and **Paúl da Serra**. Standing in front of the information board and looking across at the steep escarpment in front of us, it's difficult to imagine how any pathway can penetrate this almost vertical heath covered slope, but rest assured it

.. amazing views to the north ..

does - and what a magnificent walk it is!

Signed by a fingerpost 50 metres east along the road (Wp.2 3M), our trail follows **Levada do Lombo do Mouro** for a short distance to its source below beautiful waterfalls, sparkling against the black rock face (Wp.3 15M). A few metres ahead, the trail begins the 128 metre ascent up a rugged stairway, passing through heath forest to arrive at a mountain ridge above. The gradient is steep, with rocky uneven steps, but is well protected where necessary. Approaching the

Madeira Orchid (Dactylorhiza foliosa)

top of the ascent, the entire **Ribeira Brava** basin can be seen far below us, and rounding the last few steps (Wp.4 40M) amazing views to the north also come into view. We have our first glimpse of **Pináculo**, a rocky outcrop lying below **Bica da Cana**; we head towards it, now following **Levada da Serra**.

The heath forest along this stretch is wonderful, and during the summer months the Madeira Orchid (Dactylorhiza foliosa), although classified a rare endemic species, can be found in profusion. Also flourishing are Geranium palmatum, Canary Buttercups (Ranunculus cortusifolius) Mandon's chrysanthemums (Argyranthemum pinnatifidum) and Pride of Madeira (Echium candicans), in fact, in July along this stretch alone, we counted over twenty endemic flowering species on one visit; the contrast of colour creating a wild garden landscape (Wp.5 52M).

Another ten minutes and the trail brings us to the foot of **Pináculo** (Wp.6 62M), also referred to as Madeira's Sugar Loaf Mountain due to its elliptical shape. It's a lovely spot to take a rest on one of the stone seats arranged in the clearing.

Moving on, we follow the water channel as it heads west below **Bica da Cana**, skirting a number of semi-circular rock amphitheatres where waterfalls crash down over the *levada* into the chasms below (Wp.7 71M). Once described as a dangerous section, the paths here have recently been re-laid and protected with strong fencing. After another twenty minutes walking, first passing stone steps on our left (Wp.8 81M) that lead to more waterfalls, we reach the start of the *levada* (Wp.9 83M). A little further along a signed path appears on our right (Wp.10 103M) for the ascent to the **Bica da Cana** Forestry Post.

Approaching the water keeper's cottage

Ignoring this and passing along, we continue to follow the woodland path, a section of an ancient north - south route, which descends the valley to meet with a wide earthen track at **Caramujo** (Wp.11 145M). This leads down from **Estanquinhos** Forestry Post on **Paúl da Serra** to **Ginhas** above **São Vicente** and, turning right to descend the track, it then takes us around 45 minutes to

Casa dos Lavaceiros and Levada do Norte

reach **Levada do Norte**. A few minutes before reaching the water channel we see a water keeper's cottage (Casa dos Lavaceiros), nestling in the forest to our left.

The landscape at this point changes dramatically, while on a sharp bend in the track our route turns right to meet the *levada* and another newly restored water keeper's cottage, sitting on the edge of the channel (Wp.12 193M). Our trail follows the water's flow heading into the area of **Folhadal**, named after the endemic Folhados or Lily of the Valley trees (Clethra arborea), found in abundance here. Growing to 7 metres, their masses of upright clusters of fragrant white flowers are easy to spot between August and October along the tree canopy. Over the next few kilometers our trail leads us through a vast area of dense, green and exotic primeval forest which at intervals opens up to provide wonderful views down the **São Vicente** valley. This is the most exciting part of the trail, so have your torches at the ready, as we are about to begin negotiating the six en-route tunnels carved through the mountains. Although they often make for uncomfortable walking, they are reasonably dry and level underfoot except for a few short muddy sections.

The first tunnel (very short, around 10 metres) is soon followed by the second (Wp.13 213M). The caved entrance sits beside a cleft in the rocks and on entering we descend a few eerie steps to join the channel inside the tunnel. Around 300 metres long, it takes 10 minutes to walk through.

The caved entrance to the second tunnel

Emerging on the other side, we immediately reach the third tunnel (225M) sitting on the edge of a deep gorge and waterfall; slightly longer, it takes fourteen minutes to pass thorugh (Wp.14 240M). Both tunnels are quite narrow and low in places, but they are straight and the exits at the far end can be seen. Nevertheless, care is needed as we inch along between the rock wall and the water channel. Before arriving at the fourth tunnel, a track appears on our left (Wp.15 245M), which descends a stairway into the valley below. We ignore this to continue following the *levada* which soon veers off left before circling right into a deep forested valley. Ten minutes after passing the steps, we now arrive at the entrance (Wp.16 255M). This is one kilometer in length, but has slightly more headroom and width, making progress a little quicker. Twenty minutes later we emerge into a pretty area with another lovely waterfall to our right and deeply forested slopes to our left. The fifth tunnel is more of an archway and does not require a torch (Wp.17 285M). The final 300 metre tunnel is encountered after a further ten minutes walking (297M), taking us under the **Encumeada Pass** to emerge at a junction of the **Norte** and **Rabaças Levadas** (Wp.18 312M).

Arriving on the south side of the pass, the vegetation and climate are noticeably different. Turning left here, our route continues for fifteen minutes on a manicured stretch of the *levada* shoulder with superb views of **Pico Grande** and the **Ribeira Brava** valley to our right. Fifteen minutes along, after passing another *levada* keeper's cottage on our left, our walk ends at the information board in **Boca da Encumeada** (Wp.19 328M). A few steps lead down to the ER228, across which is **Snack Bar Encumeada**. Rounding the road junction to our left, there's a busy gift shop and *miradouro* on the ER110. From here we have a choice of taking a taxi, hitching a lift (always plenty of tourists around) or returning on foot to our starting point.

Fanal, on the north western of the **Paúl da Serra** plateau (1130 metres above sea level) is an area of immense beauty and tranquility where green grassy slopes, low shrubland and the heath and laurel forests converge. Popular for family picnics and barbeques at weekends and on public holidays, it's also an area for escaping and enjoying nature at its best.

Levada dos Cedros

Levada dos Cedros was built in the 17th century and excavated along the right hand bank of the **Ribeira da Janela** valley; it's said to be one of the oldest water channels on the island. The whole trail passes through well-conserved primitive forest, a wonderfully tranquil route with only bird sounds and trickling water to break the silence. Bathed in dappled sunlight, our path passes through lush vegetation, the canopy ensuring lots of shade even in the height of summer. Though some sections of the descent are steep, the pathway is well-laid with wooden steps to carry us down to the *levada* around 250 m below.

Access by hire car or taxi: follow the ER110 from **Encumeada** to the **Paúl da Serra** crossroads taking the ER209 north, signed 'Fanal & Ribeira da Janela' and continue for 8.1 kilometres to the start of the walk; this is signed on the left of the road just before the **Fanal** Forestry Post.

Leaving the information board (Wp.1 0M) we go down a few steps soon finding a stone cairn on our left. At first the trail descends through an area of heaths but soon transcends deep into the natural forest with its high canopy and dense vegetation.

As our descent gets steeper (Wp.2) it becomes a series of steps which wind down to eventually cross a well-constructed rustic bridge (Wp.3 14M) before continuing down further flights of steps. These eventually become a steep zigzag from where we can hear the river as it tumbles down rocks at the source of the *levada*. We descend a little further, keeping an eye out to the right, where we now see the channel below us. Soon we reach the *levada* at the bottom of the final descent, from where our route takes a short detour to the left to a strong flowing stream tumbling down beautiful waterfalls, which first feeds into the *levada* before continuing deeper into the valley below, to join the **Ribeira da**

Janela (Wp.4 28M).

We now retrace our steps to now follow the *levada* downstream, the valley to our left getting deeper. However all precipitous sections are well protected with sturdy fencing and, other than short descents, the water channel now maintains height as it clings to the forested valley side beside the rock face and the dense vegetation. A little further along we arrive at a stream at the head of a deep side valley (Wp.5 37M), from where the *levada* now flows in a northerly direction soon arriving at a semi-circular paved area at the head of another valley.

.. a pretty viewing platform ..

Continuing, we next encounter a flight of steps to our left leading to a pretty viewing platform on a rocky outcrop, again well-constructed and protected (Wp.6 50M); we can take in fine views down the **Ribeira da Janela** valley, and also pick out the ER110 running along the ridge from **Fonte do Bispo** towards **Santa**.

Following the *levada* once more, we round a side valley where another break in the forest provides us with a wonderful view of the distant forested slopes around **Galanho**.

Passing between sun and shade, the conditions along this trail are perfect for the many endemic species that thrive here, including the pink Madeira Orchid and bright yellow Giant Crowfoots, these attracting many butterflies, which flit in and out of the vegetation.

The trail now crosses another bridge in a deep side valley (Wp.7 56M) and soon we arrive at a small

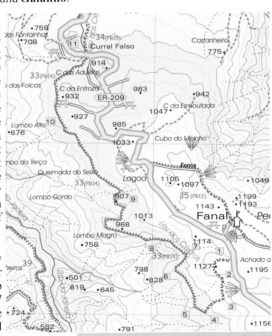

A Chaffinch

stream tumbling down the black basalt rock into the *levada* (Wp.8 62M).

Along these shady damper banks of the water channel, Liverworts, European Chain Fern and Madeira Hog Fennel also find the perfect habitat.

Continuing, we eventually arrive in a semi-circular area at yet another small valley head, where stone seating has been provided and where we can rest and partake of our refreshments (Wp.9 92M). The *laurisilva* is home to many of the island's resident bird population and sitting quietly here, the less shy species of finches, wagtails and blackbirds often make an appearance.

Suitably refreshed we continue on, crossing the final rustic bridge over a gully (Wp.10 115M) then another stone seat behind the *levada* and, with not far to go, we soon pass a stone cairn, which appears on our

.. the final rustic bridge ..

Curral Falso

right. Immediately after this steps lead us down to the ER209 regional road (Wp.11 135M) at **Curral Falso**, the end of the trail; Walk 34 (PR15) starts on the opposite side of the road beside another information panel.

Ribeira da Janela, **Porto Moniz**'s smallest parish, takes its name from the largest of three rock stacks (**Ilhéus da Ribeira da Janela**) rising 57 metres out of the sea, the natural rock aperture in its centre resembling a *janela* or window. Predominantly a wine producing area, the village extends from the mouth of the river of the same name to an altitude of 400 metres, its houses scattered among traditional agricultural terraces of sweet potatoes, beans and maize and other crops. It also boasts Madeira's only camp site, close to the river's mouth.

Ribeira da Janela 'Rockstack'

Our trail (between 840-400 metres) follows an ancient footpath used by local people to bring wood, essential to their daily lives, from the forested area above. It also connected the settlement with the south side of the island, mainly **Calheta** and **Ponta do Sol**, where wine was traded for other products.

Although the total descent on this route is 440 metres, it is gradual and without extremes in gradient.

3 | 1¼ H | 2.7 km | neg / 440m | 1

Access by hire car or taxi: follow directions for Walk 33, continuing north on the ER209 for a further 4 kilometres. The walk starts on the right of the road, beside an information panel; parking is available on the roadside.

Starting at the information board on the regional road (Wp.1 0M), we pass a stone cairn on our right and descend a wide woodland path to follow the **Levada dos Cedros** for a short distance before channel and path separate; the water channel can still be heard on the next short section. We soon meet up with the regional road (Wp.2 8M) crossing over to pick up the path on the opposite side then, a little way ahead, crossing it once again.

We continue on the path, now wide and grassy, paralleling the water channel, though again this can only be heard and not seen. Descending down wooden steps we rejoin the *levada* and here get glimpses of the coast through the low tree line. Crossing the regional road for the last time, we first go right before turning left a few metres along to continue on the trail (Wp.3 23M). Descending from the road, the path narrows where vegetation closes in; soon the *levada* crosses our path so we step over it.

Here the water channel goes off to our right, after which our route meets up with a broad forest track (Wp.4 27M) where we first turn right before picking up our trail again a few metres on the left.

The next section is a little overgrown, the character of the vegetation changing with taller pines and eucalyptus sharing space with the heath trees. Stepping down another staircase, we meet a junction with a dry stonewall where a gap in the wall is fenced off with rustic posts. We turn right, following the path for a few metres before it swings right again, now bordered by rustic posts and wire fencing. Soon we reach a few wooden steps at the bottom of which is a rudimentary gate on our left, almost indistinguishable from the fencing (Wp.5 40M). Attention is needed here as this can easily be missed, although by looking left at the bottom of the steps, the path on the other side of the gate is quite obvious.

We go through the gateway, descending yet more wooden steps. Our route soon leads us to a junction with another wide dirt track which we follow right, continuing round a bend to a point just before a stream crosses the track (Wp.6 51M). Our route goes off to the left down another wooden stairway, passing a waterfall on our right before descending again quite steeply.

The path and steps here are very narrow but soon the forest opens up, giving us our first views of village and the coast to the north. To our left are views of the southern slopes of the **Ribeira da Janela** valley, the line of the well-known walking route **Levada da Ribeira da Janela** (Walk 39) clearly visible along the forested slope.

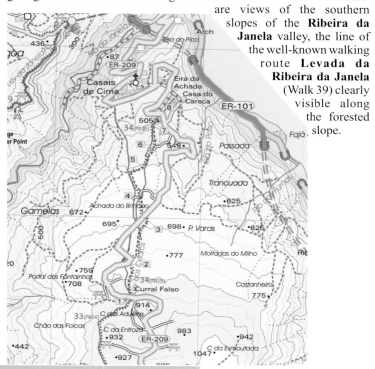

Himalayan Ginger

Along the next section we find the beautiful endemic Lily of the Valley trees as well as colourful colonies of Montbretia and Himalayan Ginger and emerging from the woodland, we now have clear views of the village nearby.

Soon after we meet another dirt track, which we again take right but almost immediately our narrow path heads off left through the grassy banking (Wp.7 63M), descending steeply and eventually passing a wooden farm building with a tin roof, before descending a few steps to the end of the route at the ER209 (Wp.8 75M).

The view from Bar Achada

The end of the walk is close by the village of **Ribeira da Janela** so following the regional road for approximately 600 metres we arrive at **Bar Achad**a, for rest and refreshments, and from where a taxi can be arranged to take us back to our starting point.

long and rather steep stairway, we find ourselves in a lovely wooded valley dominated with Besom and Tree Heath as well as Madeira Bilberry (Vaccinium padifolium) (Wp.9 118M). It's an ideal place to stop for lunch and be entertained by the Madeiran Firecrests chirping and flitting between the bushes.

Continuing, we soon cross a well-constructed wooden bridge over a small stream bed (Wp.10) and later crossing over another rocky stream (Wp.11 128M), we climb the path on the opposite banking. At the top of this ascent we meet with another path which leads off left into the valley (Wp.12 142M) but ignoring this, we keep straight ahead, soon dropping down again, where Pine and Lily of the Valley trees now appear, interspersed with the woodland heaths. A little further along we reach a picnic bench beside the path; another idyllic spot to stop for a break (Wp.13).

There now follows a 45 metre ascent, again leading us back onto and across the ER209 regional road (Wp.14 172M) our trail continuing on the opposite side. Passing through the hedgerow, the path immediately divides, our route going off to the right, but first we take a short detour left to reach a lovely viewing platform on the edge of the mountain slope, again looks down over the vast forested area to **Chão da Ribeira da Seixal**.

.. 150 stone and log steps ..

Back at the junction, the trail descends 150 stone and log steps, leading us deep into the forest below (Wp.15 180M).

The route turns left here - the section which follows is one of the best examples of primeval forest that you could wish to encounter on the island, inaccessible before the opening up of this new trail.

It's superb here; dense, dark and damp. Besom Heaths grow horizontally across the pathway, so we duck beneath; all around are ancient trees covered with mosses and lichens.

Besom Heaths

The path follows the valley side and a few minutes along, curves around a gully where in the past, a rock fall of huge boulders has shaped the landscape (Wp.16 190M). At this point protective fencing has been erected at its base but further along the path, there are one or two unprotected drops where care is needed.

Sad to leave this enchanting forest, the path soon takes us parallel with the regional road; as the road bends, our route veers off right, going between two small boulders (Wp.17). Climbing a short flight of log steps, we emerge onto a wide grassy vehicle track bordered by tree heaths.

Another kilometre along, passing yet another *miradouro* on our right, we reach a fingerboard directing us right down a narrow path through the vegetation (Wp.18 205M). At the end of the track we reach a junction with an earthen vehicle track (Wp.19 210M) and turning right, follow it down to our next fingerpost (Wp.20 215M).

At this point we are directed left along a narrow path through the undergrowth, soon reaching an old A-framed barn almost hidden in the trees; another fingerpost (Wp.21 225M) directs us left again to begin a short ascent into the forest. A number of ancient Fetid Laurels with amazing shapes and formations can be seen along this section, they are quite spectacular; if you're here at the right time of year, endemic orchids and Mandon's chrysanthemums can also be seen.

With more views down to the northern coastal area, our path eventually emerges onto a grassy plateau where a splendid high knoll ahead of us dominates the scene and the natural forest sweeps down below us.

Walking through carpets of flowers and passing beside two field code markers, our route veers off left along a narrow path before dropping down a logged stairway to lead us into the **Fanal** woods and picnic areas around the forestry post (Wp.22 245M).

This is the end of the trail, and passing beside the house we descend the driveway to reach the regional road. Another official information panel close to the gateway gives the telephone number of a local taxi service and for anyone with surplus energy, suggests linking this route with PR14 **Levada dos Cedros** (5.8 kms) and PR15 **Vereda da Ribeira da Janela** (2.7kms) ending in the village of **Ribeira da Janela** - See walks 33 & 34 for directions.

Once an important fishing centre, **Paúl do Mar** in the island's south-west still retains this tradition, though now on a much smaller scale. The overall position of the village, beneath the towering cliffs, is stunning. The prettiest and most interesting area is around the harbour and old town with its bars, restaurants and enchanting narrow streets and traditional architecture. A bronze statue on a rock looking out to sea is a tribute to fishermen past and present. Until the 1960s the only access to this village was by boat or along precipitous pathways up the sheer cliff face; now a regional road and tunnels connect the village, but only by walking one of these difficult trails can we understand the isolation of past generations.

Originally the municipal path connecting **Paúl do Mar** and **Prazeres**, this historic path makes a challenging descent contouring round the face of the cliffs, winding along steep slopes in a zigzag pattern on stone pavements and steps, recently reinstated; metal railings have been erected on all precipitous sections. The gradient is mostly extremely steep; a walking pole is recommended. There's also a total lack of shade along the whole route during summer, so it's advisable to tackle this walk either in the early morning or early evening to avoid the full extent of the sun.

Access by hire car or taxi: follow the VE3 from **Ribeira Brava** to **Prazeres** village. The walk starts at the **Jardim Atlántico Hotel** in **Lombo da Rocha** which is well signposted from the

The fingerpost at Wp.1

village centre. Parking is available either in the hotel grounds or in the overspill car park.

Access by bus: the Rodoeste Bus Nº142 from **Funchal** to **Ponta do Pargo** serves this area. Alight at **Prazeres** village.

We start at the bottom of the hotel driveway where a finger post directs us left on 'Vereda do Paúl do Mar PR19' (Wp.1 0M). Walking between the gardens and buildings we descend the hotel path with stunning views to our right, soon taking a right turn down steps between the apartment blocks to pick up the start of the trail on the cliff top. A few metres ahead, we arrive at a *miradouro* providing lovely views of the coastline and of the village of **Jardim do Mar,** nestling on a *fajã* at the base of the cliffs.

Our route begins descending, first on a wide path between abandoned agricultural terraces where a number of fig trees still remain, later narrowing after we pass a bench set beneath a small cluster of pines (Wp.2 15M). The remainder of the route follows an extremely steep gradient. Soon we have our first glimpse of **Paúl do Mar** harbour, the route quite awesome with a landscape of ochre volcanic cliffs, caves, and waterfalls. The indigenous vegetation, typical of most coastal areas in the island's west, consists mainly of Prickly Pear, Viscid Houseleek, Fish-Stunning Spurge, Globe Flower and Pride of Madeira.

We zigzag down, abandoned terraces on the western cliffs soon coming into view; how could anyone have managed to work them in such precarious positions? After two more minutes and a very steep section we have wonderful views of the harbour and pathway descending to the valley floor. On the final section of the descent we round a platform below a huge erosion in the red rock face. Swinging left, we have wonderful views of the **Seco** and **Cova** rivers falling through a cleft in the cliffs, crashing into the basin below. Soon after the gradient eases and the trail crosses a bridge over the water course where the ruins of an ancient washhouse are visible to our left (Wp.3 64M). A path leads us around the towering cliffs above the harbour. As we approach the end of the walk we pass an official information panel on our right just before a junction at the end of the path (Wp.4 72M).

Continuing left, we reach the bustling harbour. Following the road from the harbour, a short ascent past the statue of the fisherman on our left, brings us to the **Sereia (Mermaid) Pub** (Wp.5 75M) where we collapse onto chairs under a huge

.. with stunning views to our right ..

.. wonderful views of pathway and harbour ..

the fisherman statue

rubber tree. Sitting in the shade with a cold beer was

never more welcome than after this extremely hot and challenging descent.

Ponta do Pargo, a parish of **Calheta**, is the most westerly settlement on the island and logically named *ponta* (point), while *pargo* is a species of fish found in its coastal waters. The hamlets north of the village form part of this community, which has a total population of around 1250. The terrain is unlike the rest of the island, being much less forested with open countryside and rolling hills.

O Farol lighthouse

The most distinguishing feature is the manned lighthouse **O Farol**, sitting on the sea cliffs, close to which is a wonderful *miradouro* and the restaurant **Casa de Chá**. It's also an important area for Madeiran birds; many terrestrial species as well as seabirds, can be spotted.

Our circuit starts in **Ponta do Pargo**, taking in a section of the **Levada Nova** (approx 5 kilometres) to the hamlet of **Cabo**, with its picturesque headland and solitary chapel dedicated to **Nossa Senhora da Boa Morte**. The route is completed via a coastal lane through a number of rural hamlets. There's also an optional extension making a figure of eight route, taking in the lighthouse, the *miradouro* and **Casa de Chá** Restaurant.

Access by hire car or taxi: follow the VE3 to **Fajã da Ovelha** continuing on the ER101 to **Ponta do Pargo**. Approaching the end of the village, leave the regional road taking a left turn signed **Pico das Favas** and **O Farol**. A few metres ahead we meet the village road which descends to the lighthouse. Park around this junction, at a sign post on the right for **Caminho Velho**.

Access by bus:
Bus Nº142. Morning departures from **Funchal**, but return times are not convenient for walking.

From our start at the village junction (Wp.1 0M) we follow **Caminho Velho**, a concrete lane that descends off to the right and runs almost parallel to the ER101. The road contours the valley to bring us to **Pedregal** (20M) a pretty hamlet with traditional buildings and well tended gardens, where magnificent displays of Wisteria and Jasmine are found in spring. After passing a drinking fountain on the right we turn right up **Caminho do Pedregal** (Wp.2 21M), a tarred road which crosses the ER101 (Wp.3).

Crossing the road, we continue on a cobbled lane (signed 'Levada') and climb up the hill, which after the last little Madeiran house, becomes a tarred road due to the construction of the new by-pass (Via Expresso 3). The road ends in the pine and eucalyptus woodland (Wp.4) where a dirt track divides; we go left here taking the next fork right for fifteen metres to reach the *levada* (Wp.5 46M). The climb from Pedregal hamlet to the *levada* is approximately 175 metres; be aware that on a hot day it can be quite a pull.

From here we follow the channel downstream, first passing a water tank on our left and two minutes later crossing a concrete stepping bridge over a cutting and track. The *levada* now begins to sweep around two side valleys from where we have views of the lighthouse at **Ponta do Pargo** and **Pico das Favas**, a small volcanic mound with a high mast, set against a lovely oceanic view (Wp.6 58M).

Coming out of the fourth valley we suddenly arrive at a restaurant sign which points down a forest track on the left (Wp.7 83M). This comes as quite a surprise in what otherwise appears a very isolated location. The track leads to **Restaurante A Carreta**, approximately 200 metres away on the ER101, an option here for anyone wanting to take a break.

view from Levada Nova near Wp.8

Our trail continues, to sweep into a final forested valley before meeting the regional road (Wp.8 101M) which we cross over to continue on the *levada*. A further five minutes through the forest, we reach the end of the channel at a water tank on **Rua da Capela** (Wp.9 106M).

Our route goes left, descending through the hamlet of **Cabo**, soon arriving at the solitary chapel on the headland (Wp.10 116M).

.. the solitary chapel ..

It's such a beautiful spot; the original building dating from the early 17th century was rebuilt in more recent times. Nevertheless many original features remain and the architectural style is typical Portuguese.

From the chapel we follow a narrow concrete path leading down across the low grassy promontory to a *miradouro* on the edge of the cliffs (Wp.11

120M) allowing fine views along the coastline as well as providing a wonderful setting for an en-route picnic.

Back at the car park beside the chapel, we head south along an earthen track which maintains height and contours around a small valley eventually going left through the woodland. This path leads us to the hamlet of **Lombada Velha**, where we meet a tarred lane leading down from the regional road (Wp. 12).

Turning right here, we pass through the village, now back on **Caminho Velho**. After a steep descent the lane veers left to continue on to the next hamlet.

Looking to the right at the hamlet, we pass an old school house standing in a copse of date palms and eucalyptus, the latter having a shrine set into its trunk.

.. an old school house ..

Our route continues down another slope, where we cross **Ribeira da Vaca** (Wp.13) before continuing up hill to the hamlet of **Serrado**. Worthy of note at this point are the traditional Portuguese houses, many derelict and abandoned but displaying elegant and ornate carvings around the doors and windows.

Still following **Caminho Velho** as it veers off right (Wp.14 155M), we again reach **Pedregal**, passing Wp.2 to return to our starting point (Wp.1 180M). The walk from **Cabo** back to **Ponta do Pargo** is around 3 kilometres and takes approximately one hour.

Extension

Once back in **Ponta do Pargo**, you can add another circular route, either on foot or by car, to take in a visit to the lighthouse, the *miradouro* and **Casa de Chá** a lovely little tea shop and restaurant on the cliff top.

Leaving our start and finish point at the **Caminho Velho** junction (Wp.1), we descend right on the tarred road through the village before skirting around **Pico das Favas** and descending again past a number of lovely villas and the **Restaurant O Farol**, to arrive at the lighthouse on the headland (Wp.15 195M), open to the public daily offering information on this and other lighthouses around the archipelago.

Our route continues, now on the road along the headland to arrive at the *miradouro* and **Casa de Chá** (Wp.16 205M). It's open daily throughout the year (except Mondays). Continuing left, the road now leads up to **Ponta do Pargo** church in the village centre (Wp.17 225M); going left again, we return to our starting point (Wp.1 240M).

Allow one hour for this 4km extension which then makes this route 4 walker for effort and with ascents and descents of 170 metres.

Only opened to the public in 2008, **Levada do Moinho** is as yet quite unknown to most visitors, thus providing a peaceful and tranquil route along this beautiful stretch of the north-west.

Also known as **Levada Grande**, **Levada do Moinho** (The Mill Levada) had several water mills along its course, fed by the *levada*. Though in ruins, three of these remain, the best preserved being adjacent to **Achadas da Cruz** where the channel can still be seen feeding into an arched access below the building. Originally privately owned, it was built for irrigation purposes by landowners of the **Pico Alto** area of **Santa**. Beginning at **Ribeira da Cruz** close to the boundary separating the municipal areas of **Calheta** and **Porto Moniz**, it continues in a northerly direction to **Junqueira**, a small hamlet close to **Lamaceiros** where the well-known trail of **Levada da Ribeira da Janela** begins.

Access by hire car or taxi: the walk begins at a stile on the ER101 approximately 2 kilometres south of **Achadas da Cruz**, a parish of **Porto Moniz**.

Access by bus: though routes 80, 139, & 150 run to **Porto Moniz/Santa** areas, services are irregular and slow so are not recommended.

We start the trail on the ER 101 regional road where an information panel has been erected in the hedgerow (Wp.1 0M). Crossing a stile, the path ascends a flight of steps heading up the eastern side of a narrow valley, soon emerging onto a ridge giving views of the **Ribeira da Cruz** valley and the coast to the west.

.. entering the natural forest ..

We go left, following the path up the ridge, soon entering the natural forest. Climbing up by pathway and wooden steps, we reach the top of our ascent at a T-junction with the *levada* (Wp.2 25M) and turn right, following the *levada* upstream to its source.

Eventually we reach a lovely waterfall and crystal clear pool (Wp.3 38M) surrounded by lush vegetation; a further 5 minutes along we reach the *levada* source at a second waterfall (Wp.4 43M). We retrace our steps, passing our inward path now on our left, (Wp.2) and continue following the flow of the water course on to a flight of steps on the left (Wp.5 68M) where we leave the *levada* by descending the steps. (If we had carried on following the channel past Wp.5, we would eventually have found the water tumbling down the rocks to meet up with the channel at its lower level.)

At the bottom of the steps we pick up the *levada* again at a small valley head where the water tumbles into a pool from above and rejoins the channel. The forest is dense, shady and humid; in summer, endemic orchids can be seen. We reach a point where a tiny stream passes underneath the *levada*, after which we eventually emerge from the

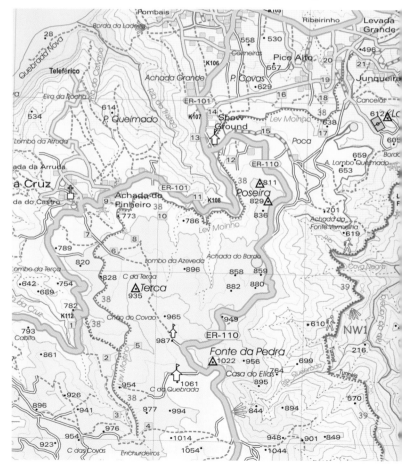

laurisilva into a more open area. It's quite overgrown here so be prepared to have a fight with the brambles and bracken (long trousers are definitely recommended along this stretch). Continuing on, we reach a short section of concrete shoulder (Wp.6 95M) before continuing on to reach a broad forest track, which comes up from the ER.101 (Wp.7 100M).

Across the track, our route leads us over a stile and along a grassy section of path, soon reaching a point where the *levada* veers off right, then again descends rapidly to a lower level. From here we follow a wooden stairway which zigzags down and swings left at the bottom before taking a right (Wp.8 108M) down another stairway, to arrive at one of the ancient water mills. Originally the *levada* could be directed through the mill but now rejoins the concrete channel a few metres to the left.

Our trail has again entered natural forest and begins to circle around **Achadas da Cruz**, soon arriving at a flight of steps on our left and a water treatment building on our right **Reservatória Achadas da Cruz** (Wp.9 122M). The steps lead down into the village and anyone wanting to take a short break here can find refreshments at a snack bar in the centre.

Leaving the steps and the water treatment building, we continue through the *laurisilva* from where the *levada* path becomes a wild garden setting (depending on season) with a number of large flowering species, which although originally introduced, have flourished in this humid environment; Passion flower from S. America, large yellow Ginger Lilies from the Himalayas, Montbretia from S. Africa and European Fuchsia adorn the route. Unfortunately, whilst a delight to the eye, these are all extremely invasive species, considered to be a threat to Madeira's endemic flora.

On leaving the forest, the water channel soon passes through a large area affected by fire damage in 2007 in the process of being cleared at the time of writing, the upside of which is that we enjoy good views of the coastline.

Walking through this section, we arrive at a point (Wp.10 129M) where the *levada* again falls away, while we follow more wooden steps down to the lower level. Passing through the centre of the clearing, our route soon leads us back into natural forest (Wp.11 136M) and continues on through lush vegetation around a number of deep ravines, rocky features and waterfalls. The gorges along here are deep but all are protected with metal fencing. We are in the habitat of the Long-toed Pigeon (Columba Trocaz) one of only two Madeiran endemics. These shy creatures escape above the canopy when disturbed, giving us only a glimpse of fluttering wings.

Soon we pass a cairn on our left and immediately after leave the *levada* on steps to the left, reaching the ER110 at the **Santa** Forestry Post (Wp.12 160M). Refreshments are to be had at **Bar Santa**, found around 400 metres away by turning right at the T-junction visible to our left.

Our final section starts at the Forestry Post, but is a little more confusing

At the Santa forestry post

so adherence to the detailed directions is essential.

Our route leads us past the front of the forestry house before taking a right turn at the end of the driveway onto **Caminho do Pico** (Wp.13), a grass and sandy path skirting the perimeter of the Agricultural Show Ground.

Walking along here, we soon re-join the *levada* where it gushes down a small waterfall into the channel (Wp.14 166M). In another few metres the *levada* is joined by a secondary channel, both running parallel for a short distance before separating again at a point where the track veers off to the left (Wp.15). Our channel leaves us here for a short distance but can be heard as it courses down through the woodland.

Meeting up with the levada again

We follow the track left for just a few metres before taking a right turn on a narrow path through a gap in the hedgerow, just before a concrete farm building, and a little distance ahead we meet up with the *levada* again where it falls down a pretty waterfall into the channel.

Now a little overgrown, our path makes a steep descent, eventually levelling out (Wp.16 176M) to emerge alongside an agricultural area above **Pico Alto**.

The overgrown section before Wp.17

Continuing, our trail soon crosses a concrete road, then progresses through a densely overgrown section making navigation sometimes difficult; obviously this is less so during winter, but summer walkers need to ensure that they keep close to the *levada* in order to find the correct route.

Fortunately, this is only a short section and we soon reach a stile, with another a few metres along (Wp.17. 186M) which then leads us into the woodland.

Another few minutes, and the channel splits. Here we go left, descending beside the main channel which is continual and fast flowing.

A little further along the *levada* falls away to the left while we continue behind a farm building descending steps (Wp.18 192M) and passing between more buildings to re-join it at the bottom.

We descend a tarred road to the right for a few metres. Here the *levada* flows at a slightly higher level on our right; we meet up with it again going right up a short concrete drive (Wp.19 200M), following it between old agricultural houses and buildings, beautiful in August, interspersed with meadows of red flowering Montbretia.

.. meadows of red flowering Montbretia ..

Another slightly tricky section follows (Wp.20). Here the *levada* is first on our left so we step across to follow it downwards on our right until we emerge at a concrete shelter on the right. Here a newer channel flows left, but we go straight on, following the old channel down to a concrete road. We cross over diagonally to the right to rejoin the *levada* where we continue for a few minutes, taking in wonderful views of the north coast before descending a flight of steps leading down to the roadside in **Junqueira** (Wp.21 210M).

The **Ribeira da Janela** gorge is most impressive, both from the head of the valley around **Rabaçal**, down to its mouth at **Ribeira da Janela** and the *levada* of the same name. **Levada da Ribeira da Janela**, constructed in the early nineteen-sixties, extends fifteen kilometres into the impressive **Janela** gorge, providing unforgettable views on almost every step of the way.

Leaving Fonte do Bispo (Wp.1)

The most popular access point is from the village of **Lamaceiros** above **São Vicente**, where the first few kilometres of the channel follow a well-manicured path lined with agapanthus, hydrangea and other exotic species. For those wanting a gentle stroll, this is the best option.

However our chosen route, offering the most spectacular approach into the valley, starts at **Fonte do Bispo**, (1235 metres) from where the trail descends 760 metres through the area of **Galhano** before meeting the *levada* close to is source below **Rabaçal**.

This exhilarating walk descends from high altitude vegetation, then heads deep into the natural forest, skirting high cliffs and waterfalls as it passes through eight tunnels on its way to **Lamaceiros**. It takes about two hours (around 5 kilometres) to reach the *levada* on a continual descent which gets considerably steeper towards the end, where large sections of the path and steps, particularly in winter, are quite dangerous due to leaf litter, so care is needed; the authors consider a walking pole to be essential.

| 4 | 6H | 17 km | | neg. 763m | | 3 | 1 |

Access by hire car or taxi:	**Alternative access**
follow the ER110 regional road across **Paúl da Serra** to the second junction with the ER210 **Prazeres** road. The walk starts across from the junction, where a wide track signed 'Galhano', leads into the valley.	Leave **Porto Moniz** on the ER-101 on a zigzag climb up the escarpment before turning left towards **Lamaceiros**. Continue through the village and follow the signs to the *levada*, parking at the barbeque and picnic site adjacent to the water station and reservoir.
Access by bus: Nº139 One bus daily leaves mid-morning from **Funchal** via **Encumeada** and	Bus Nºs 80 &150 go to **Porto Moniz**. Taxis are available for the onward route to **Lamaceiros**.

Fonte do Bispo. No return service.

Starting on the north side of the regional road (Wp.1 0M) we follow a wide vehicular track signed 'Galhano', soon crossing a cattle grid and stream to arrive at a signpost indicating 'Vereda do Galhano'. Passing through denser vegetation with occasional views of **Fanal** across the valley, we then meet another signpost with a grassy clearing to the right; from here our track becomes a single footpath (Wp.2 80M). A little further along we cross a bridge over a fantastic rocky gorge and, winding around the foot of a cliff to our right, the trail begins to zigzag steeply before arriving at the *levada* (Wp.3 110M). Once on the channel shoulder, two fingerposts appear, one indicating that it's twelve kilometres to **Lamaceiros** following our route, while the second signpost shows the way to the *levada* source, three kilometres east. This is an option for anyone wanting to extend the walk, or for a shorter detour of around 150 metres; there's a small water house with a kitchen refuge, a good place to stop for lunch or for shelter if needed.

Now beginning the second section of the trail, we head off west following the water flow and prepare ourselves for the eight tunnels. The longest of these is 1200 metres and a number are wet underfoot and overhead, so waterproofs and torches need to be at the ready. We are soon at the first tunnel (around 200 metres long) and although there's plenty of headroom and the going is good underfoot, the path slopes slightly whereas the tunnels to come have a protective wall between the path and channel.

Emerging, we find ourselves in a deep wooded gorge before entering the second and longest tunnel (130M).

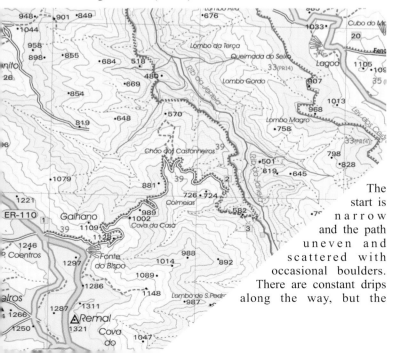

The start is narrow and the path uneven and scattered with occasional boulders. There are constant drips along the way, but the

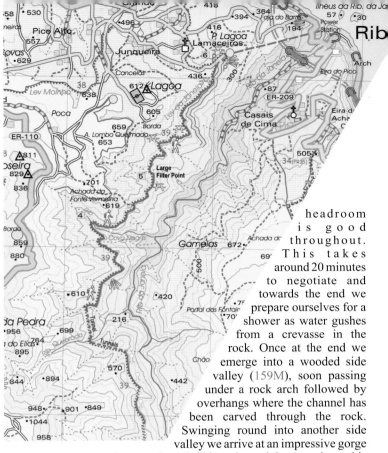

headroom is good throughout. This takes around 20 minutes to negotiate and towards the end we prepare ourselves for a shower as water gushes from a crevasse in the rock. Once at the end we emerge into a wooded side valley (159M), soon passing under a rock arch followed by overhangs where the channel has been carved through the rock. Swinging round into another side valley we arrive at an impressive gorge (161M) where the path veers sharp left then sharp right to navigate this section. The channel is now on our left and whilst some stretches are quite precipitous, these are protected with metal railings.

A little further along we pass behind a waterfall (169M) followed by more steep sections protected only by a flimsy wire barrier, so care is needed. However, the magnificent views up the valley and the fantastic gorge to our right more than compensate. The third tunnel is short; after exiting (180M) we soon reach the fourth tunnel (around 80 metres long) with low headroom and a narrow path (184M). Emerging into the daylight (187M), the *levada* now makes a large loop around another waterfall where again the path is quite narrow but well protected, where we enjoy more stunning views.

An easy stretch of path follows before arriving at the fifth tunnel (206M), around 50 metres in length with low entrance and exit (208M). The sixth tunnel (211M), around 200 metres long, has good headroom throughout although there are rock projections in a couple of places. Emerging (217M), we sweep round to the right to arrive at the **Levada House** (223M), a quiet and pleasant place to stop for refreshments. We are likely to be joined by many chaffinches, so used to walkers that they have become quite tame.

The route near Wp.16

From the house, it is around five kilometers to **Lamaceiros**. The next section of the *levada* is cut against the rock walls where overhangs drip onto the path and, with little space along this ledge, the channel here is covered with concrete slabs; this section is quite precipitous but hand rails have been provided for security (240M). The seventh tunnel (243M) is short but curved, with the end only visible from the halfway point. The path is also very wet but there is good headroom.

At the exit we find ourselves above a deep gorge where a most spectacular waterfall cascades over the *levada* for us to pass beneath (245M). Even if you walk the alternative route from **Lamaceiros**, you'll hopefully decide to make it to this point to enjoy this magnificent gorge. Rounding the arc of the gorge, we enter the final tunnel, slightly less than 200 metres in length and again wet and muddy, but a reasonably good path. Emerging, we find ourselves in a beautiful wooded area (260M) where the channel shoulder is narrow but the *levada* is again paved. Along this final stretch to **Lamaceiros** there are a few short precipitous sections but these are very well protected.

Continuing, the path passes over a large water run-off area with wonderful views of the valley and the river bed below (Wp.4 300M), and soon after reaches the first of three picnic areas, with views down to the coast at **Ribeira da Janela** (Wp.5 320M); the terraced slopes and houses of the village of **Ribeira da Janela** also come into view across the valley.

Eventually passing through pine and eucalyptus woodland, we reach a tarred road which we cross over to follow the channel as it sweeps left towards the **Lamaceiros** water station and the end of the trail (Wp.6 360M).

This pretty and extremely popular location is likely to be busy whatever the time of year. The excellent facilities, recently built, include a number of covered barbeque areas, picnic tables and toilets with a bar also nearing completion.

Barbeque at Lamaceiros

The *levada* network is probably Madeira's greatest tourist attraction, with over 200 channels criss-crossing the island's basalt rock masses, enabling penetration into otherwise impenetrable areas of the interior. **Levada Fajã do Rodrigues** is no exception and this particular trail leads us into one of the rarest areas of the laurisilva. To say it is spectacular is an understatement; perhaps the following quote from Raimundo Quintal, a local environmentalist and author, is more apt. "The Ribeira do Inferno valley is the work of the Creator, and there the Great Architect of the Universe excelled Himself".

This exhilarating trail passes along a mountainous ledge and through four en-route tunnels. However, as it's quite challenging and exacting, walkers need to be sure-footed and wear appropriate footwear and clothing; have good torches at the ready. We guarantee you won't be disappointed.

The *levada* shoulder is reasonably wide and level and is culverted in a number of places. There are a few slippery sections along the route and though protective railings have been erected these were found to be broken in places, so care is needed. The tunnels present the most difficulty where they are particularly narrow and low overhead, albeit well constructed and level underfoot. We found these sections quite uncomfortable; however, there's the alternative of walking in the water channel, which is quite shallow.

Those wanting a more leisurely stroll could undertake the first thirty minutes of the main trail to the valley head and waterfall, returning from there to the starting point to pick up the additional route, another 30 minutes each way.

Access by hire car or taxi: from **Ribeira Brava** follow the VE4 to **São Vicente**. At the first roundabout after the tunnel, take the second right on the old regional road and after 500 metres take a left turn signed 'Ginhas e Lanço'. Continue for 3.4 kilometres up the hill, keeping left at two junctions following the signs for Parque Empresarial de São Vicente. As the tarred road ends a wide gravel track ascends to a water collection station and water keeper's cottage approx 400 metres ahead. The track is accessible by car; alternatively park at the end of the tarred road.

Access by bus: routes N°s 6 & 39 from **Funchal** & **Ribeira Brava** to **São Vicente** – transfer by taxi to **Ginhas.**

Levada Fajã do Rodrigues, also know as **Fajã da Ama**, lies in an upland area of **São Vicente** and is one of the recommended walking routes signed

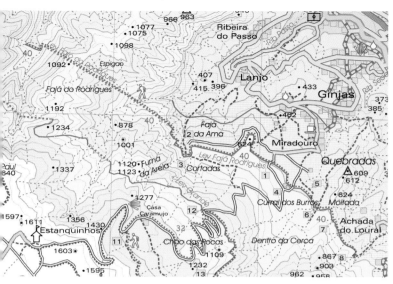

and opened by the Forestry Service in 2006. Across from the information board along the track (Wp.1 0M) a finger post directs us on to the *levada*, first passing between large water tanks on our right and the water keeper's

The eastern mountain range, from Ginhas

cottage a little higher on our left. This first section is well planted with flowering shrubs and the shoulder is wide and comfortable as it passes a sluiceway cascading down on the left, before entering pine and eucalyptus woodland.

Levada Fajã do Rodrigues

Now gently strolling, we pass two straight rows of huge cedars and soon encounter a track on our right (Wp.2 15M) before rounding into a deep valley where, in front of us now, appears an impressive waterfall which drops down from the wonderful forested peaks above. At this point the trail has entered the natural forest; crossing the narrow valley head (Wp.3 24M), it now clings to the horizontal rock face before taking us round a deep arc and under another waterfall to arrive at the first tunnel entrance (38M). Around 40 metres long, it takes only a few minutes to walk through. A few metres ahead, after enjoying lovely views down the **São Vicente** valley, we enter the second tunnel of around 300 metres. Here the discomfort begins as we inch along crab fashion, section by section. However relief awaits us at around the half way point where stone slabs have been laid across the channel - now progress is

The second tunnel entrance

much easier. Emerging into the light (46M) we soon find ourselves in a damp, lush and narrow side valley.

Our trail heads towards the valley head, passing a river and pools down to our left, before meeting a 10 metre tunnel followed by a concrete plinth leading across the rock face to the entrance of the fourth 1000 metre tunnel. Inside the shorter tunnel and after scrambling over a sluice gate, an amazing cavern opens up on our left, at the back of which is a wonderful waterfall dropping into a crystal clear pool at our feet. Crossing over the plinth and rounding the water run off, we now enter the longer tunnel, which due to its length, becomes extremely uncomfortable as we make slow progress along the channel.

.. rare, wild world ..

Fortunately its last 200 metres are again culverted, but the roof is still quite low in places and water drips from above in a number of sections. It's at this point that you might begin to question why we're doing this, but the answer soon unfolds as the trail emerges into the rare and wild world of the **Ribeira do Inferno** valley (83M).

We are on the edge of a deep, green forested bowl resembling a huge crater. Indigenous vegetation extends from the valley floor up the towering slopes, the wild species forming a dense canopy of Til, Madeira Mahogany, Canary Laurel, Lily of the Valley, Picconia and Dogwood, plus a lush mass of smaller endemic laurisilva species.

Along this section, the channel and path are carved into the rock and run around the rim of the valley; looking down, we can see the river bed snaking along the valley floor. It is incredibly damp, humid and exotic here, the rock face a mass of lichens, liverworts and grasses all dominated by great chain ferns, creating tunnels from the overhanging rocks. It's magnificent; the discomfort of the tunnels is now forgotten as we take in the beauty of this isolated location.

The path around this valley is reasonably wide and well protected with metal fencing, although sections are very slippery where water drains down into the valley below. Rounding the next bend and passing beneath overhanging rock, the walk ends as it reaches **Ribeira do Inferno** and the source of the *levada* (90M).

Being no other way out of this valley, we now retrace our steps back to the starting point (Wp.1 180M). On beginning the journey back, one of our party decided to walk in the *levada* channel through the long tunnel and doing so, made up twenty minutes on the rest of the party. This is a good option for taller and heavier built people, or anyone carrying a heavier backpack (which is really not recommended). The channel is very even underfoot and the water, although quite cold, is only between two and six inches in depth.

Additional Route (1 hour return + 3km)

From the information panel (Wp.1 0M) the *levada* can be followed downstream as it crosses the area of **Fajã da Ama** to **Achada do Loura**, where it then enters a long tunnel taking water down to the Hydro Power Station at **Serra da Água**. A few metres from the start, the *levada* path is joined by a wide track as it passes between two cottages with agricultural plots and apple groves (Wp.4 5M) after which, a path leads off to a viewing platform above the **São Vicente** valley. Soon the track veers off to the left (Wp.5 10M) and from here we continue to follow the *levada* path, now entering into the natural forest on the eastern slopes.

Wide and comfortable this pretty stretch is lined with hydrangea, Pride of Madeira and other flowering species. Occasionally the trees open up to provide stunning views of the eastern mountain range across the valley (Wp.6 15M).

Another few minutes along, we reach a picnic table (Wp.7 25M) followed by another picnic area a little further along before arriving at the tunnel entrance (Wp.8 30M), not accessible to walkers. This is the end of the additional route and here we turn round and head back to our starting point (Wp.1 60M).

.. the trees open up to provide stunning views ..

All waypoints are quoted positions using the WGS84 Datum in Latitude and Longitude format.

For notes on using GPS on Madeira, see pages 22 and 23.

GPS records for these routes are available on our PNFs (Personal Navigator FIles) CD, available from Discovery Walking Guides Ltd.; for more details, see www.walking.demon.co.uk or www.dwgwalking.co.uk

Digital download versions are also available at www.instant-books.org

1. The Socorridos Valley - Western Funchal

Wp	North	West
01	32 39.5475	16 57.0785
02	32 39.5145	16 57.1015
03	32 39.5925	16 57.2245
04	32 40.0675	16 57.2335
05	32 39.9755	16 57.4555
06	32 40.2195	16 57.4095
07	32 40.2905	16 57.4045
08	32 40.5315	16 57.4115
09	32 40.6955	16 57.3585
10	32 40.8295	16 57.3505
11	32 39.4395	16 57.3185
12	32 39.6295	16 57.4175
13	32 39.6655	16 57.4555
14	32 39.6285	16 57.5775
15	32 39.5095	16 57.6425
16	32 39.2345	16 57.7345
17	32 39.3365	16 57.5525
18	32 39.0615	16 57.5845
19	32 39.0335	16 57.5085

2. Eira do Serrado to Curral das Freiras (Nun's Valley)

Wp	North	West
01	32 42.6335	16 57.7295
02	32 42.6715	16 57.8635
03	32 42.7835	16 57.7915
04	32 42.7955	16 57.8815
05	32 43.0375	16 57.8095

3. Boca da Corrida to Encumeada (PR12 Caminho Real da Encumeada)

Wp	North	West
01	32 42.6575	16 59.2125
02	32 42.6425	16 59.1655
03	32 43.2435	16 59.4275
04	32 43.3455	16 59.4105
05	32 43.3615	16 59.3485
06	32 43.8555	16 59.1475
07	32 43.9865	17 00.0085
08	32 44.2095	16 59.9975
09	32 44.4005	17 00.0885
10	32 44.3865	17 00.3505
11	32 44.6355	17 00.2585
12	32 44.7075	16 59.8945
13	32 44.8715	17 00.7175
14	32 44.8745	17 00.9715
15	32 45.2065	17 01.2495

4. Ecological Park - Ribeira das Cales to Monte to Babosas(PR 3.1 Caminho Real do Monte)

Wp	North	West
01	32 42.0785	16 54.1955
02	32 41.8935	16 54.2595
03	32 41.7125	16 54.2165
04	32 41.5755	16 54.1785
05	32 41.6505	16 54.2125
06	32 41.5235	16 54.0265
07	32 41.4525	16 53.9895
08	32 41.3455	16 53.9785
09	32 41.1135	16 54.0515
10	32 41.0485	16 53.9715
11	32 40.7475	16 54.0495
12	32 40.6275	16 54.1225
13	32 40.6055	16 54.1745
14	32 40.5235	16 54.1455
15	32 40.5385	16 54.0355
16	32 40.5685	16 53.9515

5. Ecological Park - Poço da Neve to Chão da Lagoa to Ribeira das Cales (PR 3 Vereda do Burro)

Wp	North	West
01	32 43.5535	16 55.4815
02	32 43.4575	16 55.4185
03	32 43.4395	16 55.3015
04	32 43.4225	16 55.0885
05	32 43.2945	16 54.9425
06	32 43.2515	16 54.9015
07	32 43.0785	16 54.7965
08	32 42.9095	16 54.4225
09	32 42.6685	16 54.3705
10	32 42.6415	16 54.3255
11	32 42.6115	16 54.2785
12	32 42.4165	16 54.3145
13	32 42.2935	16 54.3055
14	32 42.2005	16 54.2515
15	32 42.2155	16 54.1805
16	32 42.0475	16 54.2645
17	32 42.0615	16 54.1855

6. Ecological Park- Poço da Neve to Levada do Barreiro to Ribeira das Cales (PR 4 Levada do Barreiro)

Wp	North	West
01	32 43.5555	16 55.4805
02	32 43.4595	16 55.4175
03	32 43.2355	16 55.3645
04	32 43.1575	16 55.1955
05	32 42.9465	16 55.0165
06	32 42.9085	16 54.9825
07	32 42.7825	16 54.9575
08	32 42.6925	16 55.0555
09	32 42.4885	16 55.0635
10	32 42.3885	16 55.0405
11	32 42.1575	16 55.0215
12	32 41.8795	16 54.8085
13	32 41.7975	16 54.7315
14	32 41.7965	16 54.6835
15	32 41.7475	16 54.6025
16	32 41.7365	16 54.5145
17	32 41.8435	16 54.2645
18	32 41.9995	16 54.2735
19	32 42.0595	16 54.1845

7.
Levada dos Tornos - Monte to Babosas to Curral Romeiros

Wp	North	West
01	32 40.5975	16 54.1815
02	32 40.5895	16 53.9465
03	32 40.6795	16 53.7605
04	32 40.9765	16 53.7025
05	32 41.0055	16 53.6455
06	32 40.5985	16 53.5785
07	32 40.6675	16 53.6035
08	32 40.7555	16 53.6415
09	32 40.5195	16 53.5345
10	32 40.5505	16 53.4625

8.
Romeiros to Horténsia Tea Rooms and Lombo da Quinta

Wp	North	West
01	32 40.5505	16 53.4625
02	32 40.5895	16 53.3635
03	32 40.5885	16 53.2505
04	32 40.5775	16 53.1285
05	32 40.3515	16 53.3725
06	32 40.3035	16 53.4015
07	32 40.2195	16 53.1895
08	32 40.1065	16 53.0905
09	32 40.0585	16 53.0745
10	32 40.1455	16 52.8855
11	32 40.0355	16 52.8595
12	32 39.9915	16 52.7655
13	32 39.9855	16 52.5315

9.
Lombo da Quinta to Camacha

Wp	North	West
01	32 39.9855	16 52.5315
02	32 39.8685	16 52.0855
03	32 39.8595	16 51.9925
04	32 40.0395	16 51.9435
05	32 40.0085	16 51.7075
06	32 39.9045	16 51.6455
07	32 39.9785	16 51.5295
08	32 39.9415	16 51.4825
09	32 40.0015	16 51.4765
10	32 39.9005	16 51.1285
11	32 40.0175	16 51.1735
12	32 40.1745	16 51.1645
13	32 40.1175	16 51.0705
14	32 40.1765	16 50.9045
15	32 40.0845	16 50.7805
16	32 40.0665	16 50.6435
17	32 40.0355	16 50.5175
18	32 40.0825	16 50.5315
19	32 40.1095	16 50.5675
20	32 40.7855	16 50.7315

10.
Vereda da Ponta de São Lourenço (PR08)

Wp	North	West
01	32 44.6035	16 42.0555
02	32 44.6695	16 42.0415
03	32 44.8195	16 41.8845
04	32 44.8405	16 41.8585
05	32 44.9215	16 41.8515
06	32 44.9095	16 41.7685
07	32 44.9325	16 41.7735
08	32 45.0075	16 41.7455
09	32 45.0235	16 41.6955
10	32 45.0345	16 41.6666
11	32 45.0266	16 41.6444
12	32 44.9815	16 41.6225
13	32 44.9185	16 41.6055
14	32 44.9375	16 41.5255
15	32 44.7955	16 41.4375
16	32 44.7815	16 41.2566
17	32 44.6895	16 41.1715
18	32 44.6255	16 41.1885
19	32 44.5615	16 41.1505
20	32 44.5305	16 41.1675
21	32 44.5515	16 41.1015
22	32 44.4785	16 41.0395
23	32 44.5185	16 41.0055
24	32 44.5725	16 40.9105

11.
Pico do Facho to Machico

Wp	North	West
01	32 43.9695	16 45.8475
02	32 43.5444	16 45.5695
03	32 43.4395	16 45.5075
04	32 43.4366	16 45.5544
05	32 43.5155	16 45.6325
06	32 43.5315	16 45.7085
07	32 43.4244	16 45.8515
08	32 43.1185	16 45.5555
09	32 43.1615	16 45.8675

12.
Levada do Caniçal (East)

Wp	North	West
01	32 44.2255	16 45.4555
02	32 44.2944	16 45.3325
03	32 44.3985	16 44.9025
04	32 44.6035	16 44.9295
05	32 44.7655	16 44.9475
06	32 44.8635	16 45.0995
07	32 44.8955	16 44.9355
08	32 45.0305	16 45.0444
09	32 44.9905	16 44.7235
10	32 45.0535	16 44.6544
11	32 44.5185	16 44.2566
12	32 44.2435	16 44.3005

13.
The Old Trail to Caniçal

Wp	North	West
01	32 43.9655	16 45.8544
02	32 43.5415	16 45.5705
03	32 43.7585	16 45.2644
04	32 43.8295	16 45.2925
05	32 43.8785	16 44.9875
06	32 44.0834	16 44.8255
07	32 44.1825	16 44.7955
08	32 44.1135	16 44.7344
09	32 44.1355	16 44.4075
10	32 44.2444	16 44.3025

14.
Boca do Risco from Túnel do Caniçal

Wp	North	West
01	32 43.9825	16 45.8595
02	32 44.2815	16 46.3675
03	32 44.5805	16 46.3144
04	32 44.7705	16 46.4015
05	32 44.9505	16 46.3525
06	32 45.0115	16 46.2255
07	32 45.1485	16 46.1866
08	32 45.2515	16 46.2266
09	32 45.3344	16 46.3485
10	32 44.6095	16 46.4395
11	32 44.5644	16 46.5115
12	32 44.4585	16 46.4935
13	32 43.9825	16 46.4495

15.
Portela - Maroços (PR05 Vereda das Funduras)

Wp	North	West
01	32 44.8515	16 49.5144
02	32 44.7525	16 49.0725
03	32 44.8105	16 48.8644
04	32 44.9575	16 48.6875
05	32 45.3135	16 47.9905
06	32 45.3444	16 47.9295
07	32 44.9005	16 47.7405
08	32 45.0025	16 47.3844
09	32 45.0015	16 47.6805
10	32 44.8634	16 47.8135
11	32 44.8066	16 47.8715
12	32 44.6755	16 47.8166
13	32 44.6455	16 47.8485
14	32 44.6574	16 47.8975
15	32 44.4766	16 47.8344
16	32 44.3215	16 47.8655
17	32 44.2485	16 47.8833

16.
Levada do Castelejo

Wp	North	West
01	32 46.0305	16 51.0505
02	32 46.0705	16 51.1485

03	32 45.9705	16 51.1455
04	32 45.8195	16 51.2425
05	32 45.5215	16 51.2266
06	32 45.2055	16 51.2277
07	32 45.0475	16 51.3866
08	32 44.6455	16 51.7077

17.

Arco de São Jorge to Boaventura

Wp	North	West
01	32 49.4785	16 57.6105
02	32 49.5695	16 58.0177
03	32 49.5255	16 58.1905
04	32 49.5977	16 58.2715
05	32 49.5225	16 58.2166
06	32 49.5315	16 58.3405
07	32 49.6185	16 58.3825
08	32 49.0585	16 59.2495

18.

Areeiro to Ruivo (PR01 Vereda do Areeiro)

Wp	North	West
01	32 44.1115	16 55.7266
02	32 44.1395	16 55.7234
03	32 44.3535	16 56.0125
04	32 44.3466	16 56.1795
05	32 44.4705	16 56.3315
06	32 44.5944	16 56.2975
07	32 44.9444	16 55.8944
08	32 45.0215	16 55.9655
09	32 45.1185	16 56.1285
10	32 45.2305	16 56.3015
11	32 45.6177	16 56.4915
12	32 45.5266	16 56.5615

19.

Pico Ruivo to Ilha, São Jorge (PR01.1 Vereda da Ilha)

Wp	North	West
01	32 45.6744	16 56.1375
02	32 45.7977	16 56.0905
03	32 45.9825	16 55.8985
04	32 46.3166	16 55.8166
05	32 46.7133	16 55.6525
06	32 47.0695	16 55.5605
07	32 47.4805	16 55.3215
08	32 47.5755	16 55.0585
09	32 47.7355	16 54.9435
10	32 47.9195	16 54.9515
11	32 48.1825	16 54.8855
12	32 48.3533	16 54.6875
13	32 48.6777	16 54.6966

20.

Achada do Teixeria to Pico Ruivo (PR01.2 Vereda do Pico Ruivo)

Wp	North	West
01	32 45.8905	16 55.2666
02	32 45.9433	16 55.1305
03	32 45.8825	16 55.5133
04	32 45.7966	16 55.6833
05	32 45.7933	16 55.9466
06	32 45.6733	16 56.1395
07	32 45.6655	16 56.2044
08	32 45.6325	16 56.3477
09	32 45.6095	16 56.4615
10	32 45.6195	16 56.4915
11	32 45.6095	16 56.6015
12	32 45.5277	16 56.5577

21.

Pico Ruivo to Encumeada (PR01.3 Vereda da Encumeada)

Wp	North	West
01	32 45.6095	16 56.5977
02	32 45.5744	16 57.2033
03	32 45.5625	16 57.4666
04	32 45.6266	16 57.8185
05	32 45.5185	16 58.1444
06	32 45.2985	16 58.5605
07	32 45.2544	16 58.7605
08	32 45.2844	16 58.9077
09	32 45.1785	16 59.2415
10	32 45.2544	17 01.1095

22.

Levada do Caldeirão Verde (PR09)

Wp	North	West
01	32 47.0485	16 54.3315
02	32 47.1144	16 54.4366
03	32 46.9855	16 54.7985
04	32 46.8455	16 55.0305
05	32 46.7355	16 55.3295
06	32 46.9005	16 55.3415
07	32 47.0925	16 55.3725
08	32 47.0815	16 55.5085
09	32 46.8025	16 55.8725
10	32 46.5677	16 56.1515

23.

Ribeiro Bonito (PR18 Levada do Rei)

Wp	North	West
01	32 49.0185	16 55.4795
02	32 48.9505	16 55.5225
03	32 48.7785	16 55.6185
04	32 48.4995	16 56.2277
05	32 48.4033	16 56.3766
06	32 48.4095	16 56.2345

07	32 48.2933	16 56.0877
08	32 48.0915	16 56.1055
09	32 47.9325	16 56.2285
10	32 47.7733	16 56.2288

24.

Vereda dos Balcões (PR11)

Wp	North	West
01	32 44.1315	16 53.1733
02	32 44.1777	16 53.2915
03	32 44.2277	16 53.2705
04	32 44.3444	16 53.3144
05	32 44.4625	16 53.3077
06	32 44.4705	16 53.3555
07	32 44.4955	16 53.4185
08	32 44.2605	16 53.5115

25.

Ribeiro Frio to Portela (PR10 Levada do Furado)

Wp	North	West
01	32 44.1044	16 53.1795
02	32 44.3233	16 52.8525
03	32 44.3295	16 52.7877
04	32 44.3033	16 52.7395
05	32 44.2915	16 52.7205
06	32 44.2333	16 52.5955
07	32 44.0366	16 52.2415
08	32 44.4333	16 51.4495
09	32 44.5266	16 51.2677
10	32 44.3744	16 50.8325
11	32 44.4733	16 50.6833
12	32 44.6255	16 50.3687
13	32 44.7105	16 49.7885
14	32 44.7275	16 49.5825
15	32 44.8366	16 49.5425

26.

Ribeiro Frio Circular

Wp	North	West
01	32 44.1044	16 53.1795
02	32 44.3233	16 52.8525
03	32 44.3295	16 52.7878
04	32 44.3035	16 52.7395
05	32 44.2915	16 52.7205
06	32 44.2334	16 52.5956
07	32 44.0366	16 52.2415
08	32 43.9766	16 52.3605
09	32 43.9485	16 52.5944
10	32 43.8676	16 52.6434
11	32 43.7655	16 52.8215
12	32 43.7277	16 52.8134
13	32 43.6444	16 53.0005
14	32 43.6387	16 53.0795
15	32 43.8315	16 53.0804
16	32 43.8685	16 53.2495
17	32 44.0215	16 53.2595

27.
Portela to Pico do Suna to Santo da Serra

Wp	North	West
01	32 44.8385	16 49.5415
02	32 44.7366	16 49.5895
03	32 44.7105	16 49.7833
04	32 44.7615	16 50.2195
05	32 44.6244	16 50.3685
06	32 44.4725	16 50.6595
07	32 44.3634	16 50.8295
08	32 44.2995	16 50.9325
09	32 44.1494	16 51.2325
10	32 44.1497	16 51.2396
11	32 44.2576	16 51.2266
12	32 44.2466	16 50.7933
13	32 44.1945	16 50.5495
14	32 43.9944	16 50.4276
15	32 43.9795	16 50.4066
16	32 43.9676	16 50.3215
17	32 43.9244	16 50.1495
18	32 43.7185	16 49.7934
19	32 43.5824	16 49.6386
20	32 43.4595	16 49.1455

28.
Rabaçal: Levada das 25 Fontes (PR06)

Wp	North	West
01	32 45.7025	17 08.0625
02	32 45.7454	17 07.9005
03	32 45.7585	17 07.7705
04	32 45.7144	17 07.5195
05	32 45.9425	17 07.5285
06	32 45.9775	17 07.7995
07	32 45.8205	17 07.8834
08	32 45.7785	17 08.1134
09	32 45.7334	17 08.1725
10	32 45.6766	17 08.1834
11	32 45.3576	17 08.5334
12	32 45.2266	17 08.9565
13	32 45.3305	17 08.0695

29.
Rabaçal: Levada do Risco (PR06.1)

Wp	North	West
01	32 45.2966	17 08.0315
02	32 45.2085	17 07.7515
03	32 45.7000	17 08.0625
04	32 45.7266	17 08.0434
05	32 45.7805	17 07.9566
06	32 45.7376	17 07.8995
07	32 45.6334	17 07.4595

30.
Rabaçal: Ribeira Grande

Wp	North	West
01	32 45.2634	17 07.9885
02	32 45.2355	17 07.9766
03	32 45.2055	17 07.9534
04	32 45.1805	17 07.6464
05	32 45.2295	17 07.5795
06	32 45.2485	17 07.6915
07	32 45.2654	17 07.7495
08	32 45.3366	17 07.8125
09	32 45.4725	17 07.8015
10	32 45.4915	17 07.5234
11	32 45.4696	17 07.2324
12	32 45.4044	17 07.0766
13	32 45.3885	17 06.8685
14	32 45.4066	17 06.8455
15	32 45.409	17 06.7344

31.
Rabaçal: Lagoa do Vento

Wp	North	West
01	32 45.4615	17 07.2355
02	32 45.5066	17 07.2234
03	32 45.5205	17 07.2566
04	32 45.5724	17 07.3915
05	32 45.5976	17 07.3415
06	32 45.6086	17 07.5715
07	32 45.5736	17 07.6786
08	32 45.6595	17 08.0144
09	32 45.6976	17 08.0685

32.
Encumeada to Pináculo to Folhadal (PR17 Caminho do Pinaculo e Folhadal)

Wp	North	West
01	32 44.5095	17 02.7766
02	32 44.5634	17 02.6855
03	32 44.7895	17 02.5015
04	32 44.8515	17 02.4915
05	32 44.9776	17 02.7615
06	32 45.1825	17 02.7695
07	32 45.1934	17 03.0775
08	32 45.3225	17 03.1834
09	32 45.3534	17 03.1855
10	32 45.6234	17 03.4725
11	32 46.2895	17 03.8955
12	32 46.4466	17 03.3475
13	32 46.0576	17 03.2834
14	32 45.7426	17 03.0044
15	32 45.6776	17 02.9255
16	32 45.4685	17 02.8515
17	32 45.2195	17 02.0085
18	32 45.0776	17 01.6955
19	32 45.2534	17 01.1555

33.
Fanal to Curral Falso (PR14 Levada dos Cedros)

Wp	North	West
01	32 48.3676	17 08.4525
02	32 48.2635	17 08.5634
03	32 48.1255	17 08.5266
04	32 47.9705	17 08.6595
05	32 48.0855	17 08.7686
06	32 48.3075	17 08.8975
07	32 48.3615	17 08.7915
08	32 48.4696	17 08.9085
09	32 48.6615	17 09.2005
10	32 49.0905	17 09.6285
11	32 49.5595	17 09.4776

34.
Curral Falso to Ribeira da Janela (PR15 Verada da Ribeira da Janela)

Wp	North	West
01	32 49.5595	17 09.4776
02	32 49.7455	17 09.4825
03	32 50.0135	17 09.4004
04	32 50.1625	17 09.4134
05	32 50.3195	17 09.4315
06	32 50.4324	17 09.3315
07	32 50.5786	17 09.3405
08	32 50.6485	17 09.3055

35.
Verada do Fanal (PR13)

Wp	North	West
01	32 46.0304	17 06.4645
02	32 46.2766	17 07.1015
03	32 46.3884	17 07.1594
04	32 46.3676	17 07.3555
05	32 46.3875	17 07.6456
06	32 46.4455	17 07.9546
07	32 46.6136	17 07.9624
08	32 46.8015	17 08.1875
09	32 46.8625	17 08.0875
10	32 46.9065	17 07.9874
11	32 46.9595	17 08.1006
12	32 47.1984	17 08.1374
13	32 47.3726	17 07.9345
14	32 47.4984	17 07.7386
15	32 47.4564	17 07.6744
16	32 47.6086	17 07.7514
17	32 47.8336	17 07.7885
18	32 48.2636	17 07.9046
19	32 48.3795	17 07.8736
20	32 48.5265	17 07.7004
21	32 48.5954	17 07.8394
22	32 48.5695	17 08.4684

36.
Prazeres to Paúl do Mar Harbour (PR19 Camino Real do Paúl do Mar)

Wp	North	West
01	32 45.1315	17 13.0105
02	32 45.2725	17 13.0825
03	32 45.1815	17 13.3456
04	32 45.1786	17 13.4385

| 05 | 32 45.1735 | 17 13.5066 |

37. Ponta do Pargo to Cabo Circular

Wp	North	West
01	32 48.8355	17 14.7715
02	32 49.1115	17 14.6644
03	32 49.0455	17 14.5454
04	32 48.8155	17 13.9395
05	32 48.8325	17 13.8375
06	32 49.0344	17 13.7155
07	32 49.4805	17 13.6677
08	32 49.5815	17 13.5466
09	32 49.7525	17 13.5405
10	32 49.9235	17 14.0866
11	32 50.0085	17 14.2234
12	32 49.5686	17 14.3085
13	32 49.3255	17 14.4175
14	32 49.2086	17 14.5884
15	32 48.8496	17 15.7744
16	32 48.5805	17 15.3885
17	32 48.7034	17 14.8605

38. Levada do Moinho to Achadas das Cruz (PR07)

Wp	North	West
01	32 49.7605	17 12.4976
02	32 49.5535	17 12.2934
03	32 49.2196	17 12.1515
04	32 49.0606	17 12.1375
05	32 49.5755	17 12.2524
06	32 50.0655	17 12.4195
07	32 50.1625	17 12.4276
08	32 50.2705	17 12.3176
09	32 50.3915	17 12.2966
10	32 50.4334	17 11.9355
11	32 50.4015	17 11.8134
12	32 50.7434	17 11.6276
13	32 50.8025	17 11.6696
14	32 50.9115	17 11.5585
15	32 50.9444	17 11.3334
16	32 51.0085	17 11.2295
17	32 50.9625	17 10.9455
18	32 51.0735	17 10.8615
19	32 51.1776	17 10.8005
20	32 51.2915	17 10.7815
21	32 51.3215	17 10.6524

39. Fonte do Bispo to Galhano to Levada da Ribeira da Janela

Wp	North	West
01	32 47.7935	17 11.0125
02	32 48.0515	17 09.7825
03	32 47.8986	17 09.5777
04	32 50.1615	17 10.8125
05	32 50.3744	17 10.4134
06	32 51.1035	17 09.9924

40. Ginhas, São Vicente to Ribeira do Inferno (PR16 Levada Fajã do Rodrigues)

Wp	North	West
01	32 46.7477	17 02.9605
02	32 46.8205	17 03.3955
03	32 46.7666	17 03.4565
04	32 46.6166	17 02.8035
05	32 46.5656	17 02.6886
06	32 46.4676	17 02.6186
07	32 46.3976	17 02.4724
08	32 46.1944	17 02.3324

Walking Route Start Coordinates

If you are using a GPS we suggest that you load the waypoints for your chosen walking route and switch it on when approaching the start of a walk. On the GPS map screen you will see yourself approaching the start point and when you get to Wp.1 you are at the start point.

For SatNav users we suggest setting your unit to 'Navigate To' Wp.1 of your chosen walk by inputting the coordinates of Wp.1 from the Waypoint Lists. If your SatNav will only accept UTM coordinates here are the UTM coordinates of Wp.1 for all 40 walking routes. All of Madeira is in the UTM Zone 28S.

Walk	Easting	Northing						
1	317005	3615179	19	318683	3626476	37	289709	3632892
2	316093	3620901	20	320050	3626851	38	293294	3634527
3	313776	3620989	21	317962	3626369	39	295535	3630844
4	321596	3619776	22	321548	3628964	40	308068	3628658
5	319635	3622538	23	319823	3632636			
6	319638	3622542	24	323260	3623540			
7	321569	3617038	25	323250	3623490			
8	322691	3616930	26	323250	3623490			
9	324127	3615860	27	328956	3624748			
10	340640	3624118	28	300062	3626886			
11	334697	3623043	29	300096	3626135			
12	335317	3623506	30	300146	3626072			
13	334686	3623037	31	301345	3626415			
14	334680	3623068	32	308274	3624517			
15	328998	3624771	33	299554	3631822			
16	326638	3626991	34	297999	3634059			
17	316513	3633547	35	302571	3627442			
18	319272	3623575	36	292313	3625988			

APPENDIX A USEFUL INFORMATION

Please note that, while the following information is believed to be correct at the time of printing, it is advisable to check on opening hours etc. on arrival. Ask in tourist offices, or your hotel reception staff may be able to help. The dial code for Madeira from overseas is + 351.

TAXIS

Calheta	291 822 423	Monte	291 782158
Estrela da Calheta 966038547	919695861	Ponta Delgada	291 862449
Camacha	291 922185	Ponta do Sol	291 972110
Cãmara de Lobos 291 942700	291942407	Porto da Cruz	291 562411
Campanario	291 953601	Paúl do Mar	963075612
Caniçal 291 961989	917323630	Porto Moniz	291 852243291 852164
Caniço 291 932156	291 933022		966045524
Canhas 291 972470	919514041	Ponta do Pargo	965013090
Faial	291 572416	Amparo	967425752
Funchal:		Cabo	291 882165
Central	291 222000	Ribeira Brava	291 952349 291 952606
Avenida do Mar	291 523473		966045604
Lido	291 741412	Ribeira da Janela	291 852166 917842059
Mercada	291 226400	Ribeiro Frio	291 782158
Martinho	291 765620	Santa Cruz	291 524888
Nazaré	291 762780	Santana	291 572540 291 572788
Ginhas, São Vicente	291 846149	Santo da Serra	291 522100
Guala	291 526643	São Vicente	291 842238 291 842929
Machico 291 962480	291962220		
	291 963666		

USEFUL PHONE NUMBERS

Emergencies	112	Motorway Assistance (VE)	800 203 040
Airport	291 520 888	Coastguard	291 700 112
Police	291 208 200	Assistance at Sea	291 230 112
Motorway Assistance(V1)	800 290 290	Red Cross (Cruz Vermelha)	291 741 115

TOURIST INFORMATION

The regional tourist offices do not always keep to their published opening times, but the main Funchal office is reliable. There's a few leaflets to take away; most publications are for sale.

N.B.Some businesses offer 'tourist information' when their aim is to sell you coach trips, hire cars or time-share. The Tourist Offices listed below are the 'official' Madeira Tourist Authority offices.

Main Tourist Office, Funchal 291 211 900/902
Direcção Regional do Turismo info@madeira tourism.org
Avenida Arriaga No 18, 9004-519 Funchal www.madeiratourism.org
Mon to Fri 9.00 a.m. - 8.00 p.m. Sat & Sun 9.00 a.m. - 6.00 p.m.
Tourist Office, Monumental Lido 291 775254
C.C. Monumental Lido, Estrada Monumental, 284, 9000-100 Funchal
Mon to Fri 9.00 a.m. - 8.00 p.m. Sat 9.00 a.m. - 2.00 p.m.
Tourist Office at Airport, Santa Catarina de Baixo, 9100 Santa Cruz 291 524933
Daily 9.00 a.m. - 12.00 p.m.
Tourist Office, Caniço, 9125 Caniço de Baixo 921 932919
Mon to Fri 9.00 a.m. - 12.30 p.m. & 2.00 p.m. - 5.30 p.m.
Tourist Office, Machico, Forte Nossa Senhora do Amparo, 9200 Machico 291 962289
Mon to Fri 9.00 a.m. - 12.00 p.m.& 2.00 p.m. - 5.00 p.m. Sat 09.30 a.m. - 12.00 p.m.
Tourist Office, Ribeira Brava, Forte de São Bento, 9350 Ribeira Brava 291 951675
Mon to Fri 9.00 a.m. - 12.30 p.m. & 2.00 p.m. - 5.00 p.m. Sat 9.30 a.m. - 12.00 p.m.
Tourist Office, Lugar de Baixo, Centro de Observação de Natureza 291 972850
Lagoa - Lugar de Baixo, 9860,110 Ponta do Sol
Mon to Fri 9.00 a.m. - 12.30 p.m. & 2.00 p.m. Sat 9.30 a.m. - 12.00 p.m.

Tourist Office, Câmara de Lobos, Town Hall 921 943470
Câmara de Lobos, Largo de Republica, 9300 Câmara de Lobos
Mon to Fri 9.00 a.m. - 12.30 p.m. & 2.00 p.m. - 5.00 p.m. Sat 9.30 a.m. - 12.00 p.m.
Tourist Office, Porto Moniz, 9270 Porto Moniz 291 825555
Mon - Fri 10.00 a.m. - 3.00 p.m. Sat 12.00 p.m. - 3.00 p.m.
Tourist Office, Santana, Sitio do Serrado, 9230 Santana 291 572 992
Mon to Fri 9.00 a.m. - 12.30 p.m. & 2.00 p.m. - 5.30 p.m. Sat 9.30 a.m. - 12.00 p.m.
Tourist Office, Porto Santo 291 982 361
Avenida Henrique Vieira e Castro, Porto Santo 9400
Mon to Fri 9.00 a.m. - 5.30 p.m. Sat 10.00 a.m. - 12.30 p.m.

THINGS TO DO Note: this list is not exhaustive.

GOLF
For general golf information see www.madeiragolf.com

Palheiro Golf, Quinta do Palheiro Ferreiro, São Gonçalo 291 792116 / 291 792456
9050-296 FUNCHAL www.palheirogolf.com reservations@palheirogolf.com
Santo da Serra Golf reservas@santodaserragolf.com
Machico www.santodaserragolf.com

HORSE RIDING & MULE TREKKING
Centro Hipico Quinta de São Jorge 291 552043
Santo da Serra, 9100-255 Santa Cruz www.quintadesaojorge.com
Hipicenter - Horseriding 967 671 689
Sitio da Ponta, 9400-085 Porto Santo hipicenter.tripod.com/1passeios.htm
Mule Trekking, Donkey Rides 913 032 310
Parque Ecológico do Funchal info@passoburro.com www.passoburro.com

DIVING
Manta Diving Center, Galaresort Hotels, Galomar 291 935588
Rua Robert Baden Powell stefan@mantadiving.com
9125-036 Caniço de Baixo www.mantadiving.com
Horizonte do Atlántico, Rua do Quebra Costas, 28, 2 291 280024 / 963 390796
9000-034 Funchal www.venturadomar.com www.venturadomar@iol.pt
Tubar Madeira Mergulho, Hotel Pestana Palms, Lido 291 794124 / 291 709227
9000-107 Funchal www.scuba-madeira.com tubarao.madeira@netmadeira.com

SAILING/WHALE & DOLPHIN WATCHING & TRIPS TO THE DESERTAS ISLANDS
Gavião, Luxury Yacht 291 241124 / 291 706401
Marina do Funchal, 9000-055 Funchal gaviaomadeira@netmadeira.com
Bonita da Madeira "Dream Cruises" 291 762 218 291 763345
Estrada Monumental 187 info@bonita-da-madeira.com
9000-100 Funchal www.bonita-da-madeira.com

SAILING/WHALE & DOLPHIN WATCHING
Beluga Submarine Vision -Glass Bottom Boat 967 044217
Visões Aquadélicas. Lda belugasubmarine@hotmail.com
Trav.Pilar, Lt6, R/c. Dt, St Antonio. Funchal aquadelic.visions@netmadeira.com
Sea Pleasure/Sea the Best - Catamarans 291 224900 / 963 796860
Prazer do Mar, Actividades Maritimo-Turisticas,Lda info@madeiracatamaran.com
Rua das Hortas 11, 2o Andar, 9050-024 Funchal www.madeiracatamaran.com
Ribeira Brava - Restored Fishing Vessel 963 103 762 291 771 582
Lobosonda, Calheta Marine, Calheta lobosonda@sapo.pt
Green Storm, Rua Santa Luzia, 83 - G 291 706401 / 919 996099
9050-068 Funchal info@greenstorm.pt www.greenstorm.pt
Santa Maria (Replica of Columbus's vessel) 291 220327
Marina - Funchal, 9000-055 Funchal nau.santa.maria@mail.telepac.pt
Sea Born, Sea Born Kiosk 291 231 312 - 919 916 221
Marina do Funchal seaborn@madeira.com

FISHING

Euromar, Avenida do Infante, 58   291 229220 / 291 200750
9004-526 Funchal   sede@euromar-travel.com
Fish Madeira, Travessa das Virtudes, 23   291 752685
9000-664 Funchal   bristow@netmadeira.com www.fishmadeira.com
Madeira Big Game Fishing, Marina do Funchal   291 227169 / 291 231823
9000-055 Funchal   madeira.fishing@clix.pt www.madeiragamefish.com
Nautisantos, Marina do Funchal   291 231312
9000-055 Funchal   nautisantos@netmadeira.com www.nautisantosfishing.com
Turilobos, Marina do Funchal   291 238422
9000-055 Funchal   sportsfishing@mail.telepac.pt
Turimar, Marina do Funchal, Loja 15   291 226720 / 291 282175
9000-055 Funchal   turimar@netmadeira.com
Turipesca, Marina do Funchal   291 231063 / 291 766020
9000-055 Funchal   turipesca.fishingcenter.braz@clix.pt
Xiphias Sport Fishing Charters, Marina do Funchal 291 280007 / 291 280007
9000-055 Funchal   xiphias_charters@yahoo.com www.geocities.com/xiphias_charters

BIRD WATCHING
Horizonte do Atlántico, Rua do Quebra Costas, 28, 2   291 280024 / 963 390796
9000-034 Funchal   www.venturadomar@iol.pt www.venturadomar.com
Madeira Wind Birds, Rua da Pena, 10 G   291 723171
9050-099 Funchal   info@madeirabirds.com www.madeirabirds.com

CLIMBING & CANYONING
Horizonte do Atlántico, Rua do Quebra Costas, 28, 2   963 390796 / 291 280024
9000-034 Funchal   www.venturadomar.com www.venturadomar@iol.pt
Parque Ecológico do Funchal   291 784 700

APPENDIX B

NATURAL HISTORY MUSEUMS, NATURE RESERVES & GARDENS, FESTIVALS & EVENTS

We advise that you check that the opening times listed below are still current by visiting the garden websites (where available) or ask in the Tourist Information Offices.

NATURAL HISTORY MUSEUMS
Museu Municipal do Funchal (Natural History Museum and Aquarium)   Tel: 291 229761
In the beautiful **Palácio de São Pedro**. Permanent exhibitions of fauna, flora and geology including fish, bird and mammal specimens, insects, plants, minerals, rocks and fossils.
          Opening hours: Tues to Fri 10.00 a.m. - 6.00 p.m. Sat & Sun 12.00 noon - 6.00 p.m.
Aquário da Madeira Porto Moniz   www.aquariodamadeira.com
Opened 2005 in the old **São João** fort next to the small harbour in **Porto Moniz**. The interior is superb, inspired by the surrounding environment.
               Opening Hours: Daily 9.00 a.m. - 6.00 p.m.. Admission 7
Volcano Centre and Caves São Vicente
Cultural and learning centre focussing on Madeira's volcanic origins. Guided tours through caves (**Grutas de São Vicente**)and lava tubes.
               Opening Hours: Daily 9.00 a.m. - 7.00 p.m. Admission 8
Núcleo Museológico - Rota da Cal (The Lime Route)   Tel: 291 842023
New museum, **Lameiros** village, **São Vicente**. Unique site of geological and botanical importance situated in a sea limestone outbreak with fossils (over 5 million years old). In an area of *laurisilva*, it attracts endemic bird species and subspecies.
               Open daily. Admission 2
Museu da Baleia (Whale Museum)   Tel: 291 961858
Situated in **Caniçal** though moving to a new purpose-built building in October 2009, the museum will be a testament to the history of whaling.

NATURE RESERVES

Parque Ecológico do Funchal   Tel: 291 784700

The information Centre offers activities and information of a recreational and educational nature including bird watching, walking routes, donkey rides & mule trekking, plus volunteering opportunities for environment projects. There's a pretty café with outside seating

Núcleo de Dragoeiros das Neves   Tel: 291 795155

Nature conservation centre close to **São Gonçalo**, east of **Funchal**, houses a small museum in the former farmhouse. Gardens dedicated to indigenous plants species of the coastal areas including a magnificent group of ancient Dragon Trees.

Opening Hours: Daily 9.00 a.m. - 6.00 p.m. No Admission Charge

Parque Florestal – Ribeiro Frio

Next to the trout farm, displaying a collection of endemic plants specific to the *laurisilva*. In summer you will find the rare Yellow Foxglove blooming, along with many other species.

Opening Hours: Daily No Admission Charge

Espaço Natural Floresta Laurissilva   Tel: 291 854033

Chão da Ribeira, Seixal, Porto Moniz

Forest Trails, restaurant/barbecue & children's attractions

Open Daily No Admission Charge

GARDENS

Monte Palace Tropical Garden (and museum)   www.montepalace.com
Caminho do Monte, Monte   *Open daily 9.30 a.m. - 6 p.m.*
Jardim Botánico da Madeira   www.sra.pt/jarbot
Quinta do Bom Sucesso, Funchal   *Open daily (not Christmas Day) 9.00 a.m. - 6 p.m.*
Quinta das Cruzes (gardens and museum)   www.sra.pt/jarbot/
Santa Clara, Funchal   *Open Monday to Friday 10.00 a.m. - 17.30 p.m.*
Quinta Vigia, Avenida do Infante
Parque de Santa Catarina, Funchal   *Monday to Friday 9.00 a.m. - 5 p.m.*
Municipal Dona Amélia Garden, Avenida Arriaga, Funchal   www.sra.pt/jarbot
Quinta das Cruces Garden   www.rpmuseus-pt.org
Calçado do Pico,Funchal   *Open Tuesday to Sunday 10.00 a.m. - 6 p.m.*
Palheiro Gardens   www.madeira-gardens.com
Palheiro Ferreiro   *Open Monday to Friday 9.30 a.m. - 12.30 p.m.*
Quinta da Boa Vista, Rua do Lombo da Boa Vista
Funchal   *Open Monday to Saturday 9.00 a.m. - 5.30 p.m.*
Orchid Garden, Rua Pita da Silva, Funchal   www.madeiraorchids.com
Open daily 9.30 a.m. - 6 p.m.
Quinta do Arco Rose Garden, Arco de São Jorge www.quintadoarco.com
                                          Open daily 11.00 a.m. - 6 p.m.

FESTIVALS/ANNUAL EVENTS

For the exact dates when each of these annual events will take place, see www.madeiratourism.org

Walking Festival	January
Carnival	mid-February
Flower Festival	2-day event towards end April
Atlantic Festival	June
Wine Festival	end August/beginning September
Festival of the Bands	mid-October
Christmas Lights/New Year Celebrations	December/January

APPENDIX C DISABLED ROUTES

"Tourism and leisure activities have become basic aspects of modern society. The right to enjoy them is a quality of life indicator and an element of social integration, just as the right to education and work.

Leisure enjoyment forms part of a satisfying human experience and is fundamental for the physical, psychological and social development of the individual. In the case of the disabled, moreover, it can be considered a vitally important factor towards complete integration."

Taken from the Tourmac website www.tourmac.info/discapacided/index the above sets out the philosophy behind this imaginative programme, which has been funded by the European Union and the contracting Governments of Spain and Portugal, who have acquired the (Joelette) cycles, so that the disabled can enjoy hiking in this part of the world.

Joelettes (adapted wheelchairs) are offered free of charge to both local inhabitants and visitors, as a means of ensuring that no member of the family needs to miss out when the rest go walking. These routes are not suitable for normal wheelchair access; use of the adapted cycles requires either previous experience, or the services of the specialized guides.

The programme, managed in Madeira by the Forestry Service in conjunction with the Fire and Ambulance Service (The Bombeiros), currently has two routes designated for the purpose, although others will be considered on request, subject to suitable terrain. These have been established and signed with the PB JOELLETTE information panels, field code markings and fingerposts.

PBTTJOELETTE - From **Portela** to **Fajã dos Rolos** (close to **Machico**)
Distance 12.6 km - Descent 165 m.
Follows and intersects with our Walk 15 (PR5 - Vereda das Funduras)

PR JOEL - **Queimados** (**Santana**) to **Pico das Pedras**
Distance 2.1 km - Descent/Ascent 20 m.
Follows the alternative route from the start of our Walk 22 (Levada do Caldeirão Verde PR9).

ROUTE FOR THE BLIND

PR JOEL - **Queimados** (**Santana**) to **Pico das Pedras**
Distance 2.1 km - Descent 20 m.
Follows the alternative route from the start of our Walk 22 (Levada do Caldeirão Verde PR9)

Contact: -
Direcção Regional das Florestas/Secretaria Regional Ambiente Recourses Naturais
Sra. Eng. Ana Sé Tel: 291 740060Fax: 291 74065

Associação dos Bombeiros Voluntários da Calheta Sr. João Alegria - Comandante
Corporação dos Bombeiros da Calheta Tel: 291 827204 Fax: 291 827392 Mob: 96 4785443

Associação dos Bombeiros Voluntários da Santana
Sr. Nuno - Adjunto do Comandante da Corporação dos Bombeiros Santana
Sr. José Antonio Freitas - Comandante Tel: 291 570110 Fax: 291
570119   Mob: 96 4786895

Casado Povo de Machico
Sr Emanuel Spinola - Presidente da Casa do Povo de Machico
Tel: 291 966098   Fax: 291 966384   Mob: 913 458384

CYCLING ROUTES

PBTTJOELETTE - From **Portela** to **Fajã dos Rolos** (eastern route close to **Machico**)
Distance 12.6 km - Descent 165 m. Follows and intersects with our Walk 15 (PR5 - Verada das Funduras)

PBTT1 - From **Cruzinhas**, **Fonte do Bispo** to **São Lourenço**, **Fajá da Ovelha** (western route starting close to the Forestry Post at **Fonte do Bispo**; off the ER210). Descent c.700m

PBTT2 - **Lombada dos Cedros** (northern route starting from **Fonte do Bispo**) - Details not available at time of printing.

APPENDIX D BIBLIOGRAPHY

MAPS

Madeira Tour & Trail Super-Durable Map (pub. Discovery Walking Guides Ltd.). Regularly re-researched and updated, highly detailed and accurate. For the latest version see www.walking.demon.co.uk or www.amazon.co.uk

Madeira Bus & Touring Map (pub. Discovery Walking Guides Ltd.). For the latest edition see websites as above.

WALKING GUIDES

Shirley Whitehead's Madeira Walks (2nd edition) (ISBN 9781904946557 pub. 2009 Discovery Walking Guides Ltd).

Companion to Walk! Madeira concentrating on lesser known and 'off the beaten track' routes particularly in the west though other areas are covered. Aimed at the independent walker, it offers gentle rambles to more challenging routes providing a comprehensive guide to each route as well as information on flora, fauna and places of interest. Includes 1:25,000 scale maps drawn from Madeira Tour & Trail Map.

REFERENCE BOOKS

Flora Endémica da Madeira (Roberto Jardim/David Fransisco pub.2000 ISBN 9728622007)

Madeira Plants and Flowers (L O Franquinho/A Da Costa pub.1999 ISBN 972917721X)

Madeira's Natural History in a Nutshell (Peter Sziemer pub.2000 ISBN 9729177317)

Madeira - A Botanical Melting Pot (Dr Susanne Lipps pub.2006 ISBN 3938282096)

SPEA - Where to Watch Birds in the Madeira Archipelago (Cláudia Delgado pub.2006 ISBN 9729901899)

Prion Birdwatchers' Guide to Portugal and Madeira (H Costa, C C Moore, G Elias (pub. Prion Birdwatchers' Guide)

Field Guide to the Birds of the Atlantic Islands: Canary Islands, Madeira, Azores, Cape Verde (Tony Clarke, Chris Orgill (Illustrator), Tony Disley pub.2006 Christopher Helm Publishers Ltd ISBN 0713660236)

A Field Guide to the Butterflies of the Ecological Park and Madeiran Archipelago (Andrew Wakeham-Dawson, Michael Salmon, António Franquinho Aguiar - published by the Câmara Municipal do Funchal

PUBLICATIONS FOR BIRD WATCHING ENTHUSIASTS

SPEA-Madeira *Discover the Birds of Laurissilva IBA (and surrounding areas)*
Discover the Birds of Ponta do Pargo IBA

- available from SPEA-Madeira (Portuguese Society for the Protection of Birds, Travessa das Torres, Old Town, 9060-314 Funchal Tel: 291 241 210 www.spea.pt madeira@spea.pt

Discover the Birds of Funchal Ecological Park Parque Ecológico do Funchal Madeira

LOCAL NEWSPAPERS AND MAGAZINES IN ENGLISH

THE BRIT

The only English language newspaper currently available. Monthly, free from hotels or 1⊡ from newsagents. Shirley contributes the regular series: 'Walking in Madeira with Shirley Whitehead'.

ESSENTIAL MADEIRA ISLANDS

A glossy leisure and lifestyle magazine produced bi-monthly by a Portuguese company, focusing on Art, Design, Fashion, Nature and Golf, as well as Eating Out. ⊡3.50 a copy.

APPENDIX E BUS INFORMATION

Madeira's remarkable network of bus services is cheap, usually punctual and is a fun way to see the island and to access some walking routes. However, finding out which bus you need can be confusing as several operators run the services, sometimes using the same bus numbers for entirely different routes. Timetable changes happen quite frequently, so use this information as a guide; pick up the latest details in Madeira's tourist offices and information/ticket kiosks along the main **Avenida do Mar**; most of the main bus stops are spread along the *avenida* or in the adjoining streets.

The main bus operator for the **Funchal** region is Horários do Funchal, offering about fifty routes. They have a special cheap seven-day ticket for a week's travel. Operators of out of town and country routes include SAM, Rodoeste, and EAC.

To get the very best out of Madeira's bus services, arm yourself with the *Madeira Bus & Touring Map* (pub. Discovery Walking Guides Ltd) which includes details of all the routes, itineraries, timetables and more, and visit www.horariosdofunchal.pt www.rodoeste.pt

ORANGE town bus route numbers/destinations:

1	Ponta da Laranjeira	23	Livramento
2	Papagaio Verde	24	Pizo (industrial zone)
3	Lombada	25	Levada de Santa Luzia (via Til)
4	Pico dos Barcelos	26	Levada de Santa Luzia (via Pena)
5	Lido	27	Caminho de Ferro
7	Travessa do Pomar	28	Dr. João
8	Santa Quiteria (via Barreiros)	29	Curral dos Romeiros
8A	Santa Quiteria	30	Largo do Miranda
9	Courelas	31	Jardim Botanico
10	Chamorra	32	Rochinha
11	Trapiche	33	Balancal
12	Jamboto (via Hospital)	34	Canto do Muro
13	Jamboto (via Viveiros)	34A	Caminho do Pasto
14	Álamos	35	Praia Formosa
15	Santana	37	Palheiro Ferreiro
15A	Achada	38	Cancela
16	Santa Quitéria	39	Montanha
16A	Pinheiro das Voltas	40	Quinta da Rocha
17	Lombo Segundo	42	Alegria
18	São João	43	Romeiras
19	Levada da Corujeira (via Pena)	44	Nazaré(via Virtudes)
19	Levada da Corujeira (via Til)	45	Nazaré (via Barreiros)
20	Monte (via Corujeira de Dentro)	46	Ribeira Grande
21	Monte (via Largo da Fonte)	47	São João Latrão
22	Babosas		

Country buses by company/colour

From/To **Funchal**

HORÁRIOS	YELLOW	SAM	CREAM/GREEN
RODOESTE	CREAM/RED	EACL	CREAM/RED

Route numbers/destinations (from Funchal)

2	Assomada	53	Faial	114	Noguiera
3	Estreito de Cãmara de	60	Boqueirão	115	Estreito da Calheta
	Lobos	77	Santo da Serra	123	Campanário
4	Madalena do Mar	78	Machico, Faial	138	São Jorge
6	Boaventura	81	Curral das Freiras	139	Porto Moniz
7	Ribeira Brava	96	Corticeiras	142	Ponta do Pargo
20	Santo da Serra	103	Arco de São Jorge	148	Boa Morte
23	Machico	107	Ponta do Pargo	154	Cabo Girão
25	Santo da Serra	110	Noguiera	155	Ponta da Oliveira
29	Camacha	113	Machico, Caniçal	156	Machico, Maroços

GLOSSARY

In addition to Portuguese words used in the text, we include other frequently encountered local words.

A

achada	plateau
aeroporto	airport
água	water
alto	high
autocarro	bus

B

baía	bay
baixo	low
bica	spring
boca	mountain pass

C

caldeirão	cauldron shaped crater or rock basin
caminho	path, country road
campo	field, plain
caniço	reed
centro de saúde	medical centre
choupana	hut, cottage
cima	above
correios	post office
cova	cavern
cruz	cross
curral	animal pen

E

estrada	road

F

faial	beech trees
fonte	spring
furado	levada tunnel

G

gaviota	gull

I

ilhéu	island

J

jardim	garden

L

lago/lagoa	lake, pool
lamaceiros	marsh land
levada	water channel
lombada	mountain ridge

M

mar	sea
mercado	market
miradouro	viewing point
monte	mountain

P

palheiro	thatched cottage or animal shelter
palmeira	palm
paragem	bus stop
pastelaria	cake shop
paúl	marshland
penha	cliff, ridge
pico	peak (mountain)
poço	well
poio	agricultural terrace
pomar	orchard
ponte	bridge
porto	port
posto florestal	forest house
pousada	government run hotel

Q

quebrada	steep slope, ravine
quinta	farm house, country manor

R

ribeira	river
risco	danger

S

serra	mountain range
sol	sun

T

teleférico	cable car
torre	tower

V

vale	valley

The following index includes place names in Portuguese and some of the most commonly used English equivalents.

PUBLISHER'S NOTE

Previous users of **Walk! Madeira** and its predecessor **34 Madeira Walks** have probably noticed the change of authors for this new edition.

David and Ros Brawn continue to research a range of walking destinations yet have passed this title into the competent hands of Madeiran residents and indefatigable walkers, Shirley and Mike Whitehead. The Brawns remain at the helm of **Discovery Walking Guides** and welcome comments and observations on any of our titles.

David & Ros Brawn

www.walking.demon.co.uk
www.dwgwalking.co.uk

ask.discovery@ntlworld.com